Kitchen to Curb

How to Start and Grow Your Own Food Truck
Business

Elliot M. Sage

Contents

Introduction

The food truck industry has been one of the fastest-growing industries in the last five years, and it is expected to continue its growth in the next decade. The high inflation rate and the rise in real estate prices forced people to look for other options. Food trucks provide a cost-effective way for anyone who wants to kick-start their own restaurant business.

If you are planning to launch your food truck business, or are simply in the early stages of considering to start one, this book is for you. You will start at the very beginning and discover the history of food trucks and how they evolved to become one of the biggest industries in the world.

You'll also learn about all the current trends so you can keep up with the ever-competitive market, and you will find an extensive market analysis to give you an idea of where the industry is now and where it will be in the next ten years.

After learning all the necessary information about the food truck business, you may want to start right away. However, there are certain things you need to do first to be prepared and guarantee a long-lasting and successful business. You will learn how to identify your niche so you can start a business based on your skills and abilities. You will also discover how to create a unique selling proposition and conduct market research for concept validation to develop your food truck concept.

Next, you will start planning your food truck. You'll find out how to write a comprehensive business plan, plan your budget and finances, and understand the legal rules and regulations to avoid any problem that may arise after you start your business.

Should you rent, lease, or buy a food truck? The book will help you uncover the pros and cons of each option to make a well-informed decision.

In addition, you'll learn how to make a layout and design your truck, develop a logo, and choose the right equipment and supplies.

This book will also show you how to build a long-lasting relationship with your suppliers, create a unique menu, market your business on social media, find the right staff, and have an efficient workflow. Just as importantly, you will learn how to choose the right location, break into the food truck catering industry, use mobile apps for orders, deal with competition, adapt to regulatory changes, and expand your business.

Food trucks play a huge role in today's culinary landscape. Not only do they allow owners to directly interact and connect with their customers, but they're also able to offer diverse options since it's easier to incorporate various trucks in one event than multiple restaurants. Moreover, they increase tourism and can grow the city's economy, as they give tourists the chance to try local food without breaking the bank. It's an exciting business, so let's get started.

Chapter 1: Understanding the Food Truck Industry

Wherever you go, there is usually a food truck standing with a long line of customers waiting to satisfy their palates. Whether you go to an event, farmer's market, or just walk around your neighborhood, you will most definitely find one. Their rising popularity has inspired people who want to get into the food industry but can't afford the costs of buying or hiring a restaurant to shift their attention to food trucks.

Young entrepreneurs find food trucks to be a great investment. They aren't as expensive as restaurants and don't require furniture, many utilities, or a big staff. Thanks to their mobility, you can always experiment with locations and take your truck to big events or popular areas.

Customers also prefer food trucks over restaurants because they make delicious food at affordable prices and offer various options with unique dishes and a fun atmosphere.

Now is the perfect time to start your food truck business. This industry is booming and has come a long way from its humble beginnings. It has now become so powerful that it can impact a country's economy.

This chapter explains the history of food trucks, their current trends and market analysis, and the opportunities and challenges of a food truck business.

Historical Evolution of Food Trucks

A bit of history first.

You may think that food trucks have come out of nowhere or are a modern invention; however, they have been around for centuries. This industry started with a Texan man called

Charles Goodnight. Charles was a famous rancher in Texas who cemented his name in history by inventing the first food truck in the world in 1866, the chuckwagon.

Charles's wagon was mainly a portable kitchen that he created for his cattle drive to suit the cowboys' needs. They spent months on the road, so he added everything to his wagon, like a water barrel, storage space, shelves, firewood, and counter space lid to cater to their needs. He either brought preserved food from home, like cornmeal, salted meat, and dried beans or gathered ingredients on the road to prepare fresh meals.

News of Charles's food truck spread all over the country, and many people in the food industry were interested in the idea. One of those was Walter Scott. He built his chuckwagon by cutting windows into it. He stood next to a busy newspaper office to sell coffee and a variety of pies to journalists.

In 1894, the industry expanded with sausage vendors setting up their wagons in universities all over the country. In 1936, a man called Oscar Mayer created the first mobile hotdog cart, which looked exactly like a hotdog. Similar to modern-day food trucks, he stood in busy neighborhoods to attract customers. In the 1950s, ice cream trucks emerged and were extremely popular.

Food carts were common on construction sites and the U.S. Army base. After the war, they started showing up in several towns. In the 1960s, chip trucks emerged. Later on, in the 1970s, many taco trucks were established around the U.S. thanks to the rise of Mexican immigrants.

However, these food trucks were expensive and didn't have the gourmet sampling or diverse menus you see in trucks today. They were basic and focused only on making money rather than creating a relationship with the customer. That and they only catered to blue-collar workers. They had a very strange name, the "Roach Coaches."

However, over the years, the food truck industry and its name changed to suit the needs of the modern age. They started selling buns with wild boar and burritos with chick-pea masala instead of salted meat and dried beans. They also expanded their clientele to people of all ages and genders and became trendier to appeal to young individuals. However, they still weren't as widespread as they are today.

So, how did food trucks become this popular in the 21st century? Things changed in the 2000s thanks to social media and a little Korean truck. In 2008, Kogi Korean BBQ created a small truck in LA selling 2$ tacos. They used social media to market their brand and announce their locations. Their food was different and tasty, a welcome break from food chains' bland and fatty burgers. These trucks were perfect for people looking for quick and delicious lunches in the middle of their busy schedules. Customers started looking for food trucks in their neighborhoods, and people in the food industry noticed the huge demand, so they started supplying them.

Technology had a huge impact on the food truck industry. Developers started creating street food apps like Roaming Hunger, Toronto Food Trucks, and NYC Food Truck. Bloggers were creating blogs, tracking and reviewing these trucks. There were even TV shows dedicated to them, like Food Truck Face-Off. Special festivals were organized for people to sample different dishes from them. Food truck owners took advantage of technology to secure licenses and manage their businesses.

Food Trucks' Current Trends and Market Analysis

Thanks to social media and entrepreneurs looking for a cost-effective way to start their businesses, the food truck industry has exploded in the last few years. Technology has provided truck owners with the opportunity to reach a wider audience. This industry has managed to not only grow and evolve but also compete with the large and powerful restaurant industry.

Their popularity doesn't seem to be slowing down either. Take a look at the current trends to have a better idea of what is going on in this rapidly growing industry.

Increased Prices and Costs

Food trucks' costs have increased dramatically in the last couple of years. COVID-19, the Ukraine War, high energy prices, and global inflation have raised start-up costs and inventory expenses, impacting all aspects of the business operation. The economic crisis around the world has affected the consumer as well as led to a disruption in supply and demand.

Food inflation has raised the prices of ingredients, forcing many restaurants to change their menus. For instance, Underbelly Hospitality had to remove their famous chicken wings from their menu due to cost fluctuations, which raised consumer prices to more than 35% of their original price.

In 2023, a food truck's start-up costs range between $50,000 to $250,000 and are expected to increase with the growing inflation. For this reason, many new food truck owners prefer to rent instead of buying trucks and starting with small menus until they make a name for themselves.

Social Media

No one can deny the power of social media in the food industry. A social media presence, or lack thereof, can make or break your business. Different platforms like X, Facebook, Instagram, and TikTok allow you to reach a wider audience and target your posts to potential customers in the area. Your target audience is determined by several factors, like your location, brand, and the type of food you serve.

Social media allows you to reach those potential customers and interact with them so you can directly market your product to them. You can also move to different locations without worrying if you will lose your customers, as you can simply notify them with a simple post. Social media also gives you the chance to build a relationship with your customers by sharing any changes in your menu or giving them a sneak peek at your operation.

Partnerships and Events

Many event organizers prefer to work with food trucks since they are basically restaurants on wheels. Partnerships with a carnival or a brewery can be beneficial for all parties involved.

Labor Shortage

One of the food industry's biggest challenges is hiring and retaining staff. The growth inflation has made the situation worse, with many restaurants closing some of their branches and letting their staff go. In the last two years, food trucks have suffered from labor shortages. Many employees feel unappreciated and undervalued due to a lack of benefits and low wages, especially compared to the conditions and long hours they must endure. A large number of restaurant employees have quit the industry for good and have no interest in returning.

However, this shortage hasn't affected the food truck industry as their sales keep growing. Many people hope that owners will start to provide fair wages and benefits for their employees to solve the labor shortage issue.

Advancement in Technology

Some people in the food industry rely on technology to fill the gap left by labor shortage. Mobile apps, websites, QR codes, and many others connect customers to restaurant employees and make the ordering process easier. Many restaurants and food trucks found that online ordering enhances customers' dining experience and makes the business's operation more efficient.

In the last couple of years, the restaurant and food truck industries faced many issues, especially during the pandemic when many people were under quarantine or practicing social distancing. Technology played a huge role in fixing many of these issues and keeping the operations running smoothly.

Food Trends

People's tastes in food change with time, and owners base their businesses on consumer trends. The last few years have witnessed a growing interest in some types of food.

- Coffee

- Juice and smoothies

- Baked goods

- Sandwiches

- Ice cream

- Grilled cheese

- Tacos

Vegetarian and Vegan Options

The number of vegetarians and vegans has grown substantially in the last few years, with many people preferring a plant-based diet over one containing animal products. When choosing their food, they usually look for vegetarian or vegan options for health reasons, personal taste, or in an effort to lead a cruelty-free lifestyle. The food truck industry is aware of this growing trend, and many have added plant-based dishes to their menu to cater to different needs.

Market Analysis

Before the pandemic, the food truck industry was growing by almost 8% a year for the last six years. Fortunately, it has remained consistent even during uncertain times like the war and inflation. People still want to dine out and order in. In fact, the rate is expected to increase in the next few years.

The global market has thrived as well thanks to the growing need for food trucks and their equipment and tools in places like Latin America and Asia, where millions of people, on both sides of the counter, rely on street food.

The rise in supply and demand and the growing popularity of food trucks have greatly impacted the food industry. However, the pandemic and inflation have caused disruptions. There was a shortage in the supply chain and an unprecedented number of job openings. Due to quarantines and social distancing, almost half of the restaurants were functioning at full capacity.

However, food trucks managed to flourish during that time. Many saw their business grow both online and offline and were even able to purchase another food truck. During a time when many restaurants were losing money, closing down, and the industry as a whole was suffering, food trucks were working at full capacity. While many of them were startups and small businesses, they were still able to stand on their feet during those tough times.

Opportunities and Challenges in the Food Truck Business

There are always opportunities and challenges in any business, and the food truck is no different. Take a look at some of the opportunities that make this business in demand.

Low-Cost

Since launching a food truck costs much less than opening a restaurant, you are potentially able to use all the money you save and invest it in other areas, such as digital marketing or creating a great menu. You will only pay for the truck's price. However, you can save a large amount of money if you rent a truck and buy second-hand equipment.

You will also pay lower taxes than restaurant owners and will need a smaller staff and fewer supplies. Trucks also don't require as many repairs and maintenance as restaurants, which saves you a lot of money in the long run.

More Customers

What's not to love about food trucks? Their foods are delicious, healthier, and safer than most street vendors. Food trucks usually attract more customers and tourists than restaurants.

Build Your Brand

If you dream of having a restaurant, food trucks will take you a step closer to achieving your goal. They allow you to build your brand before expanding and give you better control over your business. They are also perfect for first-time owners. Food trucks are more flexible since you can change location, modify your menu, or experiment with different recipes and keep changing your brand until you find your niche. This is unlike restaurants, which have a mostly fixed nature.

They also give you the opportunity to learn about the business and gain the necessary knowledge and experience before venturing into new territory.

Now, let's take a look at the food trucks' **challenges.**

Challenge 1: *Uncertain Future*

Being a business owner can be risky. You are starting a new business and don't have a stable income, and you never know what the future holds. This is especially true with food truck owners. While some people find this aspect exciting as it keeps them on their toes, others find it terrifying.

Although you can never know what the future will bring, you should still be prepared. Make sure you have a stable business that can handle the competitive market. Hire the right people, make high-quality food, and create a great experience for your clients so they always come back.

Challenge 2: *Making Sacrifices*

Success doesn't come easy. It involves hard work and a lot of sacrifices. Since you are now a new business owner, you will be solely focused on your work for the first few months. That can affect your social and personal life. You will also sleep less and have to make some financial sacrifices until your business stands on its feet. Some owners can't afford to hire staff right away, so you may perform tasks you are unfamiliar with, like marketing or interacting with customers. Your life will change drastically. For that reason, you should be prepared. It is all worth it in the end when you get to achieve your dream. Once your business becomes successful, you can hire people to do the hard work for you.

Challenge 3: *More Responsibility*

Employees only focus on one part of a business, while owners are responsible for everything. You will need to take care of sales, inventory, personnel, finding the right location, making the food, finding events, etc. Before taking this step, you should be aware of your responsibilities and be prepared for them.

Challenge 4: Competition

This industry is growing rapidly, so expect the competition to be vicious. There are new food trucks that emerge every day, some succeed, while others don't last a year. What makes yours special? How will it stand out in the market? As a business owner, you need to have a vision. Your food truck should offer something different to compete in the market.

It should cater to the consumers' needs but also be flexible in making alterations if the current trends change.

If you are planning to establish a food truck, understand that it isn't a trend or a fad that will one day go away. It is an industry that's been around for over a century. The food truck is constantly evolving and changing. This whole thing started with a wagon with window holes until it became a billion-dollar industry. One can't help but imagine what the future holds for food trucks.

Chapter 2: Developing Your Food Truck Concept

With a better understanding of how a food truck business works, you can start developing your own concept. This will be your overall theme and your main selling point, and it will set you apart from your competition. Some of the crucial factors to consider are the target demographic, cuisine, business name, main theme, logo and colors, and, last but not least, service options.

Identifying Your Niche

The first step in devising a concept for any business is identifying your niche. Remember, you'll be catering to the preferences and interests of people in specific locations, so you need to know what people living in these areas want and need. You'll find this through market analysis — the process of identifying what your target customer group is comfortable with.

Naturally, the target group will be the most profitable (the one that'll buy your products and services). Think about who will be frequenting the area and is most likely to buy from a food truck. What do they usually buy? When do they buy it (at what time of the day)? At what locations do they buy the most? You can learn this by analyzing what, when, and how your competitors sell their products and services. Is there anything your target customers would like to buy but is currently missing from the market? If yes, this could be a great opportunity to come up with a food truck concept that'll give you an advantage over the competition from the get-go. Looking for available opportunities, knowing what the competitors are or aren't doing, and grasping the target group's unfulfilled demands are crucial for establishing a successful food truck business.

With the information you gained from the market research, you can identify your niche. Once you have it, you can start developing your concept and brand. The hallmarks of a great food truck concept and brand are being unique and memo-rable, attention-grabbing, clearly expressing your intention and the basis of the concept, and, ideally, allowing for the potential for business growth.

When preparing food on a truck, you're operating with a limited space. You can only prepare the food you have space to store. Due to this, food truck businesses are typically limited to a specialty, which is what the concept is based on. However, your specialty must be aligned with market demand. Otherwise, your food truck concept won't have a strong backbone and will crumble due to lack of interest. All successful food truck concepts, like organic food targeted at health enthusiasts, fusion dishes, non-traditional gourmet sliders, and regional cuisines, are based on a strong special-ty-demand combination.

Creating a Unique Selling Proposition (USP)

The next step is coming up with a unique selling proposition (USP). In common parlance, USP is one specific reason or quality that sets your business apart from the competitors. You can use your USP to show why you're better than the competition or that you offer something they don't. For ex-ample, you might decide to make your business more ap-pealing via low prices. Or, you might sell fresh food in an area where no one else does, and your customers would welcome this opportunity. Your USP decides what your brand stands for and will be remembered by. It's not about creating a concept that appeals to everyone. It's about letting your customers know exactly what they can expect and get every time they stop at your food truck, knowing they won't get it anywhere else in the area. A strong USP appeals to people who want something only you can offer. That will help you engage them, and, coupled with quality food and services, it's what will make them come back day after day.

You'll be able to work on your USP and refine it later on, but for now, it's crucial to have an idea and a plan on how to create the most appealing proposition. Below are some pointers to help you come up with a detailed plan for creating a USP.

Create a List of Everything You Want to Offer

While it might sound counterintuitive to narrow down your niche (especially if you already have a strong idea of what your food truck would offer), making a list of everything you could sell will help you redefine some points and come up with a better USP. If all you have is a general idea of the meals you'll be cooking and selling at events and through catering contracts, it's all the more reason to make a list of every item that you think would interest your target customers. While you can start a food truck business on almost any cuisine you want, it's a good idea to create this based on meals you'll enjoy preparing for many people.

Well-tried classics often do better because people from the area enjoy it, and knowing you enjoy making it makes for an even better selling point. That said if your research shows that people from the target area are likely to try something new, feel free to include some innovative dishes as well. This is why it's crucial to write an extensive list in the beginning. You can always narrow it down later, but the more variety you have in front of you, the easier it will be to determine your USP.

Once your list is complete, take a closer look at it. Is there a meal or more than one that appeals to you in particular? Think about the menu you could create from these meals. Are they only the main dishes? If yes, what sides would go with them? Which will be your signature dish? When contemplating these questions, consider that you'll be expected to create these dishes over and over again and with the same quality and consistency. There is no point in choosing dishes you'll be tired of preparing after a while. That is more reason to only include dishes you enjoy cooking.

Make the Connections

Take a closer look at the items on the menu and see which ones you could pair together. At this point, you might still have various concepts on the table, and that's alright. With the perfect pairings, you can combine these concepts into one or a handful that could represent your main theme. Make sure to take your time to give consideration to all the pairings and relationships you can make. You never know what unexpected but mouthwatering combinations you can come up with. If you have trouble finding inspiration on how to tie the different concepts on your perspective menu together, you can always take a look at the difference in how successful food truck businesses create fusion concepts.

For example, some companies realized that certain breakfast foods sell well combined with other food items people usually buy for lunch or dinner. By incorporating, let's say, fried eggs into sandwiches, their offer does not have to be limited to one strict concept and can be something unique.

Don't worry if some of your first ideas don't make sense on their own. It's just a brainstorming phase, and you can tie everything together later on. Look for common patterns you can use to bring everything under one pile. Take your time, and when you're ready, write another list. This time, it is one that contains meals that work together and fit into one niche. If some of the items seem to be out of the main niche or contradict your USP, scrap them.

Further Competitor Analysis

It might seem like all you do when trying to create your food truck business is market and competitor analysis. However, these are fundamental when establishing a successful business and creating your USP. For example, after narrowing down your list, you might have come up with the ideal USP and concept for your business. Yet, when looking at it more closely, you realize that it isn't as special as you first thought, and you instantly lose the unique aspect of it.

During your previous market research, you've learned what customers are looking for in the target area and how your competitors are trying to cater to them. Now consider how many of these competitors are selling the same concept you've come up with in the previous step. If there are several, you don't have a USP. While many argue that operating a food truck makes the brand unique when compared to the brick-and-mortar business in the area, this simply isn't enough. Chances are, you're not the only one trying to attract potential customers with a menu similar to yours. If this second analysis shows that this is the case, start contemplating how to set your business apart.

Naturally, devising a completely one-of-a-kind concept in an area where many other food trucks are roaming the streets is nearly impossible. Your goal should be to think of something no one had before, which could significantly raise your chances of standing out from the competition. You simply have to look at what others are doing and find something about their concept that you could innovate. Here, you can consider what all the restaurants are doing and perhaps, come up with something that combines the ideas of food trucks and brick-and-mortar business. At the end of the day, your USP is about doing something better or differently than your competition — and you need to know what they're doing to come up with something they aren't doing or that you can do better or differently.

Consider the Logistics

Once you've further narrowed down your idea list, it's time to start thinking about the logistics of how you'll execute your concept. Can you prepare the proposed meals easily on the truck, or might there be logistical issues involved? Do you have adequate storage for the necessary equipment and ingredients? How long can you store the individual ingredients, and in what condition? Some items might require you to acquire additional cold storage. How long will it take to prepare the individual dishes, and how many of them can you reasonably prepare simultaneously? How much will it cost you to prepare the meals on average, and how many of them you need to sell to break even? Answering these and similar questions will help you determine whether your concept can work.

As a general rule of thumb, it's always better to start with a simple concept that involves a few menu items, as this is easier to advertise, plan, and create. You'll need fewer ingredients to buy and store, fewer meals to prepare, and lower chances of something going wrong. This way, you can channel your energy into creating the signature dishes that'll bolster your USP.

Conducting Market Research for Concept Validation

As great as your initial food truck concept may be and as unique as the proposition you've come up with after looking at your competitors' offerings is, it still needs to be validated. Otherwise, you'll either risk not offering what the customers truly want and need, or the idea will remain an idea. Many people come up with a great concept only to sit on it until someone else successfully executes it a few months later. However, if you're afraid to make this step, this is all the more reason to validate your concept. It will give you the push you need to start the business you've dreamed of for a long time. Below are some pointers on how to validate your food truck concept.

Always Look for Feedback

Don't be afraid to ask people what they think of your concept. Start with people you trust that will give you honest feedback. Sometimes, they won't tell you what you want to hear, but what you need to. Take note of what they say, and if they think your concept isn't as great as you might have thought, it's time to make some changes.

Develop an MVM

If you aren't sure whether the dishes you've chosen for your central theme fit into your concept, run a few small taste tests. For this, you'll need a small mobile food stall and an MVM (Minimum Viable Menu) people can order from. Three to four items will suffice for the initial trial. A mobile food stall can help you decide whether people will actually like what you'll be offering, especially if you're offering something new you think is missing from the market. Design the meals with perfect presentation and reach out to family and friends for feedback on the taste and look of the meals. If they don't like the latter, you can always improve your presentation skills. If they would never order the meals in general, it's time to find some new items to put on your menu or change your concepts overall, depending on how big of a role the scrapped meals play in it.

Build Your Identity

The next step in validating your food truck concept is to start building an identity and a brand around it. The few items you've chosen and validated through testing can become old news very quickly, despite how loved they might be. In this day and age, not many people want to eat the same food all the time. They want variation, and by including a few additional (special) items into your concept, you can build a brand that can survive the fickle nature of today's market.

Another reason you want to build a brand as part of your concept validation is that you're likely not the only one contemplating the same idea. If you stick with a small-scale concept, someone else will soon come, put their own spin on it, and will become far more successful. However, by coming up with a strong brand tied to your concept, you can create your own success story by being the first on the market instead of letting someone else steal this title.

Once people start validating your concept, do further research — this will help spread the news about your concept and brand. Ask for even more feedback. For example, you can tell your newly established follower base on social media what food they would like to see on your menu.

Once you have validated your food truck concept, you can move on to devising a customer acquisition plan — the next step in converting your idea into reality. You're now ready to get your menu rolling, but you still have to figure out how you'll get it to the customers and how you can establish a solid customer basis. With a preliminary (and validated) concept in mind, you can move on to planning the menu in more detail. Yes, your USP will do wonders for attracting customers in the first place, but the hardest part of the work is yet to begin. The smaller details (and, most of all, your commitment) are what will help you engage customers and obtain their assistance in establishing and running a successful food truck business.

Chapter 3: Planning Your Food Truck Business

The secret ingredient to success when it comes to launching your food truck business is planning. Without a solid plan, you're driving blindfolded through the culinary world. Why is planning a big deal? Well, the food industry is not just about what's on the menu. It's about knowing what your clients like, improvising on the spot, ticking all the legal boxes, and making waves in the foodie landscape.

The planning you make is a roadmap upon which your food truck business will run. This plan you make is not just a boring checklist but a toolkit for success that can enable you to tackle the messy bits and pieces, from the legalities to the logistics. It must be crafted to serve as a go-to for everything from procurement to the plate. It's a no-brainer that every food business aims for smooth operations, building a killer brand, and leaving customers happy. A well-thought-out food truck plan is your recipe for a business that includes these objectives and much more.

Comprehensive Business Planning

Creating a comprehensive business plan is crucial in establishing and running a successful food truck. This detailed roadmap lays out the path on which your business will thrive. It provides a bird's eye view of your venture, highlights the strategies to follow, and the financial support mechanisms that aid in securing help from potential investors or lending channels. Here's a comprehensive plan for a food truck business for inspiration. Although most common points are included in this business plan, anything can be added or omitted to tailor it according to your food truck business **(*please see Appendix for a more detailed food truck business plan template*)**.

Executive Summary
• Begin with brainstorming to compile a concise overview of your food truck business. The overview must contain the basics, like your goals and the concept or theme you'll follow.

• Work on finding the problems or the gap in the market that your food truck can address and thrive on.

• Identify your unique selling point, which you will use to inform your customers how your brand is different from the competitor and the perks it offers.

• Include an overview of your financial projections and summarize the expected revenue, expenses, and profitability.

Business Description
• Here, elaborate on the concept behind your food truck, emphasizing the type of cuisine you are offering and what you aim to deliver as a brand.

• Whatever legal structure you are aiming to follow, mention it in the description and justify your actions. For example, it could be a sole proprietorship or an LLC.

• Include information about the location where you will be setting up the food truck. Share insights like the demographics, the routes customers can use to reach you, and the competition in the area.

• Build a narrative that shares the story behind your food truck and explains its origin and your passion for the venture.

Market Analysis
• Conduct a detailed analysis of the food truck industry in your target location, considering trends, growth potential, and challenges.

• Provide a thorough competitive analysis, identifying direct and indirect competitors.

• Evaluate competitors' strengths and weaknesses and highlight opportunities for differentiation.

This market analysis will enable you to connect with your ideal customer.

Organization and Management

• Outline the organizational structure of your food truck business, specifying key roles and responsibilities.

• If you have already assigned roles, introduce the key team members, including their qualifications and relevant experience.

• Discuss your hiring strategy, detailing the skills and attributes you seek in employees.

Note: You can hire advisors or consultants who can contribute to the market analysis, organization, and management.

Products and Services

• Present a detailed menu, including descriptions of each item and its variations. You'll be adding more variations or items as your customer base grows.

• Highlight your signature dishes or delicacies that set your food truck apart.

• Point out how your menu connects with the current food scene in the area and the uniqueness it offers.

Marketing and Sales Strategy
• Develop a comprehensive marketing plan, incorporating both online and offline strategies.

• Detail your promotional strategies, including social media campaigns, partnerships, and events.

• Outline your sales strategy, discussing pricing models, sales channels, and potential collaborations.

These strategies are mostly handled by marketing professionals, but you will decide on the level of engagement and customers you want to approach through these sales and marketing strategies

Funding Request
• If you are seeking an investment from a bank, organization, or investors, specify the amount of funding you need and provide a detailed breakdown of how you intend to use the funds.

• Justify the funding request by aligning it with specific business needs like startup costs, working capital, or major expenditures.

• Clearly outline the terms you are offering to potential investors or lenders, including repayment terms and any equity offerings.

Funding Plan
• Detail your entire funding plan, including personal invest-ments, loans, grants, or any other funding sources.

• Provide a timeline for securing the funds and how you plan to allocate them.

• Discuss your strategy for managing cash flow and working capital, demonstrating your financial management related to the business.

Risk Analysis
• Identify the potential risks and challenges your food truck business may face, categorizing them as internal or external factors.

• Develop detailed strategies for mitigating and managing each identified risk.

• Consider creating a risk management plan that outlines contingency measures for unforeseen circumstances.

Remember, a comprehensive business plan is not only a document for external stakeholders but also a strategic tool for guiding your business. Regularly revisit and update it to reflect changes in the market, operations, and goals, ensuring it remains a dynamic and accurate representation of your food truck venture.

Budgeting and Financial Planning

Budgeting is a critical aspect of launching and running a successful food truck business. It's your financial roadmap that ensures you're not just dishing out delicious meals but also managing the costs effectively. Here's a breakdown of key considerations when budgeting.

Start-up Costs

Dive into the nitty-gritty of launching your food truck business by outlining the initial expenses. This involves a detailed breakdown of costs associated with acquiring the truck, whether through purchase or lease. Include estimates for outfitting the truck with kitchen equipment, like grills, fryers, refrigerators, ovens, and any specialized tools crucial to your menu. The cost you will spend on licensing, obtaining health department permits and any other relevant license must be included in the start-up costs. Lastly, make a list of the supplies you'll need to initially kickstart the kitchen. This will be your initial inventory of ingredients and supplies, and its expenses will be included in the startup cost.

Operating Expenses

Break down the expenses to day-to-day operational costs to keep your food truck up and running. The most common expenses are daily fuel expenses, parking fees, maintenance costs, insurance premiums, and miscellaneous costs that your food truck needs to stay on the road. If you are using a commissary or a shared kitchen space to prep your food, include it in the daily operating expenses alongside the cost of storage and cleaning.

Licenses and Permits

Make a list of permits, licenses, and regulatory compliance for your food truck business and research about inspections or certifications necessary for your specific cuisine or operating model. Keep these licenses and permits compiled in a file and readily accessible.

Equipment and Supplies

Itemize the costs of all kitchen equipment, utensils, and supplies required for daily operations. This includes a detailed breakdown of the cost of each piece of equipment, like griddles, deep fryers, and refrigeration units. Likewise, account for the expenses related to packaging, disposables, and any technology required for efficient point-of-sale systems.

Staffing Costs

If your business model includes hiring staff, provide a comprehensive breakdown of staffing costs. This should include estimated wages, taxes, and any benefits you plan to offer. Specify the roles you intend to hire for, whether it's chefs, cashiers, or support staff, and include industry-standard or competitive wage rates.

Marketing and Promotion

Elaborate on your marketing strategy by detailing the costs associated with building brand awareness. Break down expenses related to branding, promotional materials, and advertising. Specify any costs tied to social media marketing, website development, or participation in local events to promote your food truck.

Insurance

Thoroughly explore insurance requirements and costs associated with your food truck business. Break down expenses related to liability insurance, vehicle insurance, and any additional coverage necessary to protect your assets and investment.

Ongoing Maintenance and Upgrades

Provide a detailed plan for ongoing maintenance of your food truck and budget for potential upgrades or repairs. Include estimates for regular servicing of the vehicle, as well as any improvements or modifications needed to enhance operational efficiency. For example, your food truck would need a tire replacement once the tires wear out. Likewise, certain mechanical components of the vehicle or the food-preparing equipment can malfunction which will need maintenance, upgrades, or in some extreme cases, need to be replaced entirely.

Record-Keeping and Accounting

Discuss your approach to financial management by outlining the tools and processes you'll employ for record-keeping and accounting. This could involve appointing a staff member to keep records, investing in accounting software, or hiring a professional accountant to accurately track financial transactions, tax obligations, and overall financial health.

The efforts you put into financial planning will act as a foundation for a successful food truck business. The following section highlights the intricacies of financial planning in detail so you can become familiar with the process.

Revenue Projections

Start by forecasting your revenue. Estimate the number of meals you expect to sell daily, taking into account potential fluctuations based on location, seasonality, and market demand. Break down your revenue streams, considering the average price per dish and any additional income from catering or events.

Cost of Goods Sold (COGS)

Mention the costs directly tied to producing each meal. This includes the cost of ingredients, packaging, and any other materials used in meal preparation. Establish a detailed understanding of your gross profit margin by subtracting the COGS from your projected revenue.

Personnel Costs

Just like you included the staffing costs in the budgeting section, mention the personnel costs if you are planning on hiring staff. Besides the wages, write down the taxes associated with staffing and the financial benefits the business is considering for the staff. You must also include the number of employees, the roles you will be hiring for, seasonal staffing needs, and the hours of work you require for each position.

Capital Expenditures

The money you spend on upgrading kitchen equipment, purchasing a new truck, investing in technology, or anything significant that upgrades or adds value to your food truck business will be categorized as capital expenditure. You must include the costs of the assets, their expected lifespan, and the repair, maintenance, or replacement costs associated with the asset.

Debt Servicing

If you are running your food truck business using a loan or financing from an investor, include the repayment schedule in the plan. The repayment schedule must include the loan terms, the interest rate, and its processing charges.

Contingency Planning

No matter how many precautionary measures you take, accidents and low sales can affect any business. That's why you need a contingency plan to follow when things get out of hand. The plan can have an associated fund that can be utilized to make your business financially resilient in bad times. You can also include the potential risks and the strategies you can use to mitigate them.

Financial Analysis and Key Performance Indicators (KPIs)

Conclude your financial plan with an analysis of key performance indicators. Highlight metrics like gross profit margin, net profit margin, return on investment, and break-even point. Discuss benchmarks and milestones, indicating how you will measure and evaluate the financial success of your food truck business.

Dissecting and elucidating each aspect of financial planning creates a comprehensive roadmap that not only guides the day-to-day financial decisions but also sets the stage for long-term sustainability and success in the dynamic world of food truck entrepreneurship.

Regional and Regulatory Considerations

Food truck owners need many of the same licenses and permits that restaurants require, along with some additional truck vendor-specific ones. Understanding and adhering to regional legal and regulatory considerations is paramount for the success and compliance of your food truck business. Here's an in-depth exploration of the key facets you should consider.

Business Licensing
• Depending on the region and country you want to operate your food truck in, the licenses you'll need can differ. However, common licensing businesses for a food truck include a food vendor license, permits from the health department, and licenses that recognize your food truck as legitimate and compliant with the set regulations.

• Know about the complete process, including the processing fees and the license renewal procedure, according to the local regulations. A food truck business license can typically cost between $50 to $500, but application prices and terms will vary depending on your city.

Health and Safety Regulations
• Know about the local health and safety regulations for your food truck and the staff. Contact your state's Health Department for specific guidance.

• Educate yourself and train the staff to comply with handling, preparation, and storage protocols to ensure the safety of customers.

• Create and follow hygiene protocols according to the required standards. This includes adequate handwashing, maintaining the right food temperature for storage, and the sanitation practices you need to follow.

Zoning and Parking Regulations
• Depending on the location, check the zoning regulations so you can legally park your food truck without restrictions.

• Understand any restrictions on operating in residential areas, near schools, or in specific zones.

• Be aware of parking permits or restrictions that may apply to your food truck in different locations.

Permits for Public Events
• If participating in public events or festivals, inquire about special event permits or licenses.

• Understand the application process, deadlines, and the specific requirements for participating in such events.

Taxation and Accounting Compliance

• Work with a tax professional to understand and comply with local tax regulations.

• Ensure proper record-keeping for sales tax, income tax, and any other applicable taxes.

• Familiarize yourself with accounting standards and reporting requirements.

Employment Laws

• Understand local labor laws and regulations regarding hiring and managing employees.

• Ensure compliance with wage laws, working hours, and any employee benefits or insurance requirements.

• If hiring part-time or temporary staff, be aware of relevant regulations.

Vehicle Regulations

• Comply with regulations related to the operation of commercial vehicles, including your food truck.

• Make sure that your vehicle meets safety standards and any specific requirements for mobile food establishments.

• Regularly maintain and inspect your vehicle to meet safety and emission standards.

Environmental Regulations

• Adhere to environmental regulations related to waste disposal and recycling.

• Implement environmentally friendly practices, such as using compostable materials and minimizing waste.

• Be aware of noise and emission regulations that may apply to your food truck operations.

Alcohol Licensing

• If you plan to serve alcoholic beverages, research and obtain the necessary alcohol licenses.

• Keep the legal age and any restrictions on selling alcohol in certain areas in mind.

• Ensure compliance with responsible alcohol service practices.

Insurance Requirements

• Review and secure the necessary insurance coverage for your food truck business, including liability insurance.

• Understand the minimum coverage requirements and any additional coverage that may be advisable.

• Regularly review and update your insurance policies to ensure continued compliance.

Cultural and Dietary Considerations

• Be sensitive to cultural and dietary considerations in the area you operate in.

• Make sure that your menu and marketing materials respect and reflect the local culture.

• Be aware of any religious or cultural festivals that may impact your operations.

Navigating these legal and regulatory considerations requires thorough research, attention to detail, and ongoing compliance. Consulting with legal professionals or regulatory authorities in your specific region can provide valuable guidance tailored to your food truck business.

Chapter 4: Acquiring Your Food Truck

When starting your food truck business, one of the biggest decisions you'll have to make is whether to buy, lease, or rent your truck. This chapter outlines the advantages and disadvantages of each option to help you make an informed decision based on your needs, plans, and budget.

Pros and Cons of Buying a Food Truck

<u>**Pros**</u>
The advantages of buying a food truck include but aren't limited to the ones described below. In most cases, it's recommended to buy a new vehicle as used ones don't offer all the benefits below.

Clean and Polished Look
If you're buying a new or slightly used vehicle, it'll help you make the perfect first impression. Everything will look clean, and you won't have to worry about making it look presentable. It can help you attract more customers in the beginning stages as they'll be attracted to not only what you have to offer but also to your truck's clean and polished look.

No Upfront Repair and Low Maintenance Costs
When you purchase a brand-new truck, you won't risk unexpected repair costs for a good while. You'll have a reliable vehicle that'll help you deliver the products and services your customers come to you for. Thanks to your truck running smoothly, you'll have lower maintenance costs, and you can focus on staying on top of other aspects of your business.

That said, you can still opt for purchasing a used truck, but if you want to keep your repair and maintenance costs low, be careful. For example, by buying from local online classifieds, you can inspect the vehicles to see whether they'll truly fit your needs and are in the described condition. If they are, you'll gain the benefit of low maintenance costs without the disadvantage of paying higher upfront costs.

You Can Customize the Vehicle According to Your Needs

New, never-before-used food trucks can typically be customized based on the owner's needs. You can add new equipment that'll give you the best head start for your business. Moreover, if you don't want to do modifications now, you'll always be able to do them later on when you decide it's time for your business to grow and expand.

Additionally, you can buy already customized (new or used) trucks, which can be a great investment as these are built up to standards, and you won't have to worry about your modifications violating any laws or codes.

Great for Long-Term Investment

Long-term investments usually require a larger capital, and food trucks aren't any different. When you secure a larger capital for buying a truck, you're laying the foundation for long-term return. If your goal is to run the food truck for over 5 years, purchasing the truck might be the best option. You'll save tons of money in the long run, especially if you plan to do modifications further down the line. And if your food truck business is successful, owning the vehicle enables you to retain all the profits.

Cons

The disadvantages of buying a food truck, on the other hand, include the following points.

Upfront Investment

Without a doubt, the major downfall of purchasing a food truck is the higher upfront costs. Even if you're buying a new one, you'll still pay more right away than if you would lease or rent the vehicle. Food trucks cost between $50,000 and $100,000, depending on the type of equipment they have, space for different equipment, customizability, and many other factors. This is a large initial investment that might not be worth paying if you don't plan for modification or aren't sure whether you'll stick to the business for a long time.

Used food trucks are more cost-friendly than newer models and might even contain all the equipment you need. However, if this is your first time operating one, you might have trouble inspecting or navigating the equipment to see if it works properly.

Long-Term Commitment

When you buy a food truck, you're making a long-lasting commitment because you have to recoup the upfront costs you paid for the vehicle. You won't be able to trade or sell it if your plans for the business change or if you realize you need another type of vehicle for specific operations. If you do this before you recuperate everything you've invested, you'll lose a lot of money.

Difficulty Reselling

Reselling a food truck can be tricky as you may need to wait to find a buyer willing to pay the price you're asking. People are less likely to pay a higher price for used trucks, even if yours happens to be in top-notch condition. If they can find it cheaper somewhere else, they will buy it there. If you aren't willing to wait, you might lose more than half of its initial purchase price.

You'll Be Responsible for Repair and Maintenance

Even if you buy a brand new truck, when using it on a day-to-day basis, it will eventually need repairs. Maybe not the engine but crucial pieces of the equipment you use for preparing and storing the food. When you own everything, you're responsible for all the repairs and maintenance. Moreover, if you buy a used vehicle, the costs will rise quickly, and you and your clients will be inconvenienced if you have to stop operating the business on short notice. To avoid delaying repairs due to a lack of finances and cover your loss of business if you have to shut the truck down, it's a good idea to purchase business insurance, which is yet another additional cost.

Pros and Cons of Leasing the Food Truck

If you don't want to buy a truck outright, the next best option is to lease from a national truck leasing business or franchise one from a larger brand. Out of the two, leasing is the best option as it gives you more control over what you're selling (you would still operate your business with your menu and concept). Still, leasing has benefits and drawbacks, too.

Pros
Lower Upfront Costs
Leasing a truck will cost you far less than buying it. With a bit of research, you can find great deals that'll help you

put more money into other parts of your business, including advertisement and additional equipment.

Fixed Payments

Having to pay a fixed amount every month will help you incorporate your truck acquisition-related expenses into your business plan and budget. You won't need to worry about additional expenses for purchasing the truck, as the payments will remain fixed for the duration of the lease.

Added Flexibility

Leasing offers added flexibility you might miss out on when buying a truck. This might include making modifications or upgrades, selling the truck in case you decide to move out of the business, or shifting it slightly and buying a different type of truck to fit your new needs.

It's Great When You're Just Starting Out

Leasing can be an excellent alternative for newcomers. It allows you to get into the food truck business more quickly and seamlessly without making long-term decisions. If you decide that the industry isn't for you after all, you won't have to worry about recouping a large sum you already invested. You will have the flexibility of moving on whenever you feel this is the right move for you.

It Won't Break the Budget

Leasing a food truck is a great option if you don't have a large budget to start with. Instead of making a big investment, you can focus on distributing your funds to other parts of the business. The fixed monthly payments also make it easier to work with a tight budget.

Cons

You Are Making a Commitment

Flexibility notwithstanding, leasing requires a long-term commitment to paying the monthly fees associated with the lease. If your plan changes and you decide to cancel your lease, you'll have to pay a penalty. Moreover, some lease companies won't even allow you to cancel before a certain period, so you'll be stuck with the truck until then.

There Might Be Hidden Costs

Due to their inexperience and lack of research, new leases often have hidden costs, like maintenance, taxes, and insurance payments. If you haven't factored these costs into your business plan, you might run into several unexpected costs that can hinder your operations. Make sure you carefully read the lease agreement before signing it to understand what you're committing yourself to. If you want to avoid these potential hidden expenses, consider renting instead.

Mileage Restrictions Apply

Most lease agreements will impose mileage restrictions, limiting your use of the truck for a specific number of miles within a given period. Beyond being a nuisance when you want to cover a larger distance with your food truck, this can also hinder your ability to cater to your clients' needs. Some companies allow you to extend your miles, but only for an added cost.

You Must Decide if Leasing Is Right for You

Remember, by signing a lease, you're making a long-term commitment, so it's a good idea to think about whether you truly want to do this. You might want to wait a little before starting your business and gather more capital to purchase a truck instead. Or, if you have a great idea you want to implement as soon as possible, you might want to opt for renting instead.

You Must Consider and Compare Different Options

Leasing a food truck can be a little more complicated than buying one because you'll need to look into far more options. It's always a good idea to compare the offerings of several different leasing companies to find the option that best suits your needs. Some of the factors to consider and compare are the monthly payments, mileage restrictions, expiration dates, insurance availability and costs, and repair responsibility. For example, it's always best to go with a lease where you aren't required to pay out of pocket for all breakdowns.

You Must Have a Contingency Plan

Always have a plan for when your lease expires. This may involve renewing it or buying it. If you're interested in the latter, it's recommended to go for a lease-to-purchase option right from the get-go. This way, when your lease is up, you'll get to own the truck without making a large upfront investment.

Pros and Cons of Renting a Food Truck

Depending on your financial goals and business plan, renting a food truck might also be a viable option.

Pros
Lower Upfront Costs
Just like leasing, renting a food truck comes with considerably lower upfront costs than buying one. By renting the vehicle, you can save thousands of dollars and put these toward other business needs.

Flexibility
Renting also comes with increased flexibility in case your needs change or you decide to alter your business model. This can be a lifesaver if you plan to work in an area highly saturated with food truck businesses, which makes it much harder for a new company to attract and retain customers. If you opt out of the food truck business, you can walk away without having to sell a truck or break a lease. Renting will also enable you to venture into different food truck concepts and menus and use diverse locations.

No Unnecessary Commitments
Unlike leasing the truck, you're not committing to a long-term payment plan — nor are you committing to maintaining the truck beyond your needs and uses. You can terminate the rental agreement much more easily than any lease or switch to a new truck if you decide to upgrade the

business and start offering additional products and services. Moreover, you will be spared the hassle that comes with attempting to sell the truck if you decide to leave the business altogether.

Suitable for Tight Budgets

If you don't have the capital to buy a suitable vehicle, renting can still help you make your dream of running a food truck a reality. With no upfront costs, you can budget your money more efficiently.

Perfect for Short-Term Business Plans

Another similarity between leasing and renting is that the latter is also a fantastic option for those just trying out concepts or are just at the beginning of their food truck business journey. If you aren't sure how long you're going to run your company and are afraid of the potential challenges and competitive nature of business, renting a truck will allow you to dip your toes, try out the concept, and see whether it will work out for you without making a large upfront investment. If you decide it's not for you, you can terminate your rental agreement and walk away.

No Maintenance and Repair Costs

The rental agreement typically obligates the rental company or the truck's owner to pay for repair and maintenance. You won't have to worry about paying out of pocket or dealing with the headache of finding someone to do the necessary repairs.

Cons
Limited Customization
When renting a food truck, your ability to make modifications is quite limited. You can only personalize the vehicle up to a certain degree determined by the rental agreement, and that might not meet your specific needs. In some cases, you can make changes, but you have to remove these and return the truck when you terminate the rental agreement or pay a large penalty.

Expensive Rentals
Your rental fee might be higher than expected, depending on the truck's condition and the equipment it contains. The more additions the vehicle has, the higher the rental payment will be. Even if you're lucky enough to have a low rental fee, if you plan to remain in the business for a long time, the cumulative costs will add up to far more than if you've bought the truck in the first place.

Mileage Limitations
Rental companies will also impose mileage limitations, and if you exceed them, you'll have to pay a fee, or you might be penalized by having to return the rental earlier than expected.

You Must Shop Around and Compare Rates
To avoid running into unexpected costs and limitations, it's a good idea to compare the offerings of different rental companies and see which fits your needs best. Read their quotes and agreements carefully to be fully aware of what

you're signing up for.

You Must Inspect the Vehicle Carefully

It's also highly advised to inspect the truck very carefully before signing the rental agreement to ensure everything is in working order. Otherwise, you might run into unexpected repairs before you can even start your business. You can be held liable for damages not covered by the agreement, so you want to note any before you sign the agreement. This is something you wouldn't have to worry about when buying a new truck.

Chapter 5: Designing Your Food Truck

Now that you've developed a valid concept and business plan and acquired your new food truck, it's time to start designing your layout and branding. While good food truck branding starts when you're working on your concepts, you can only implement some of your ideas when you actually have the vehicle. This chapter outlines the necessary steps to designing your food truck, including the crucial elements of the interior design, logo and branding aspects, and equipment and tools you need to fully equip your new business.

Layout and Interior Design

Your vehicle's overall size will have a massive impact on how you can organize its layout. You'll be fitting plenty of equipment into a limited space, and if you have a smaller 14-foot truck, organizing it will be far more challenging than it would be in a 22-foot truck. Still, while it might take a while to decide where everything should go, it's not impossible.

The first step is making a list of all the equipment you'll be using and want to fit into the space you have. Map out the space and designate specific areas where the appliances and tools will go based on the truck dimensions. When designing the layout, remember to take advantage of the truck's longer sides by placing larger items like the refrigeration units, food prep area, cooking equipment, and storage along there. As a general rule of thumb, the refrigeration and the cooking units should be on opposite sides, so you can, for example, place the meal prep area next to the refrigeration unit on one side and the cooking and storage elements on the other. The smaller sides — the back and front areas — are best reserved for the in-and-out counter (usually placed on the back) and the water heater and sink, respectively.

Another way to take advantage of your space is by installing vertical elements like hanging racks and shelves or even a combi oven.

Here are some additional tips for mapping out the interior:

• **Refrigeration Units:** An under-counter freezer or refrigerator is great for cold storage solutions in small spaces. If you plan to store large quantities of food, it's recommended to go with special food truck refrigerators.

• **Cooking Elements:** Depending on your concept, you might get away with portable cooking appliances. This could also save you a lot of space, but if you're cooking larger quantities, it probably won't be feasible. Larger, non-portable cooking appliances will need to be installed under an exhaust hood, which is an additional element you must consider when designing a layout.

• **Prep or Workstations:** Some food truck owners like to prep their food in a stationary kitchen, which cuts down on the space and equipment they need for this in the truck. However, if this isn't an option for you, you'll need a large space (a major chunk of your interior space) for prepping and working.

• **Sink Area:** The easiest solution for cleaning up in a food truck is installing an underbar sink. You can place them under any other surface and clean them up as you go while having unrestricted access to the rest of your truck.

• **Warming and Warm Storage Equipment**: If your concept relies on fully or partially pre-prepared ingredients, install the warming up and warm storage equipment next to your cooking space. That way, you'll save energy, and the ingredients will remain fresh.

• **Storage Space:** Containers and bins work great for storing items that don't need refrigeration. They allow you to store ingredients in bulk, which is often a challenge in a limited space.

• **Register:** Keep your register near the in-and-out/serving zone where you'll be using it. If you want to save space, look into the tools you need to use your tablet or smartphone as a POS terminal instead of buying a bulky cash register system.

• **Serving Zone:** This should be an easily accessible space for both your customers and the truck's staff.

• **Ventilation:** Just like in any other kitchen, adequate ventilation is crucial for maintaining a safe workspace in a food truck. Make sure you factor in the necessary space for all the ventilation equipment you need to install.

Branding and Logo Development

Food truck branding is all about customizing customer experience. It can be as simple as using graphics, bright colors, enlarged logos, handwritten menus, or as extra as adding undercarriage and LED signs or special pieces of equipment your competitors don't have (a TV your customers can watch while waiting for and eating their food, for example). Some food truck owners go as far as adding speakers and awnings to improve customer experience.

Just like designing the concept, the goal with branding is to appear as unique as possible. Your brand should showcase what sets your food truck apart so the customer would be enticed to pick you over all the other options. You might also want to consider the reasoning behind your concept, primarily why you designed it the way you did and why you chose to present the food that way. Think about what you want to convey and what values you want your customers to see in your business. Lastly, consider your own personal traits and how they might impact your business identity. Customers are more likely to engage with a brand if they know that it expresses the owner's and employer's personal values and traits.

When it comes to specific things during the branding process, here are a few steps for successful food truck branding:

Design an Eye-Catching Name and Logo
The name and logo are the face of your food truck. You

need something descriptive and easy to remember that entices customers to return and recommend your products and services. For example, if you're serving a specific kind of burger, you can create a name that caters to customers who like it while alluding to what makes it so special. The overall goal is to define what your food truck has to offer and what sets it apart from the competition. By making a clearly defined statement with the brand's name, you can significantly improve brand recognition. In other words, by making it clear what your brand's name stands for, you're making it easier for customers to remember it.

Besides coming up with a suitable name, your first step in branding should also revolve around logo design. Your logo should be a symbol or text that carries the brand's values and represents it authentically — just like the name, mission statement, and tagline do. Designing a logo that sums all this up can be challenging, so take your time with it. The logo will be displayed on the truck, the supplies, and products you create for catering and other types of events to advertise your brand. Therefore, it also must be attention-grabbing to make customers engage with your brand wherever they see it displayed.

Define Your Mission Statement and Tagline

The next step is defining what your business is about — your mission statement. What do you aim to achieve by launching your brand? Think about your USP and what makes your brand different from other food trucks. The mission statement should reflect your USP, and so should all your other actions during the branding and business establishment process.

Your mission statement should additionally reinforce your brand's values and purpose. The next step is to create a catchy tagline. Once again, this should be something that aligns with your values, the brand's logo, name, and mission statement. Your goal is to communicate the brand's goals while making a connection through a relatable phrase.

Display the Business Website

In this day and age, establishing a brand without an online presence is impossible. Your website is part of your brand, so why not display it on your truck? This way, when your customers see it on the truck, they can go to your websites and learn more about your brand, products, and services. In other words, they will engage with the brand, which creates awareness and recognition. Moreover, having your website displayed on the truck will add more credibility to your brand. For added consistency, use the same design on both the website and the food truck.

Position Your Brand in the Market

Brand positioning is another crucial factor to consider if you want to set your brand apart. Market positioning defines how your customers remember your business and what it represents.

When it comes to food truck branding, you have several options for positioning:

• **Convenience-Based:** You can, for example, advertise fast service to busy customers on your truck.

• **Customer Service Based:** Offering exceptional customer experience can set you apart from competitors.

• **Price-Based:** Your main selling point can be the affordability of your food.

• **Competitor-Based:** Highlighting key differences from competitors or advertising what you can do better is another great branding tactic you can display.

• **Quality-Based:** Advertising superior product quality can significantly improve your potential client's perception of your food truck brand.

Present Delicious Food

Needless to say, the food on the menu plays a crucial role in establishing your food truck brand. Once you commit to a menu, stay consistent with it, as this will help you establish your brand. You can play around with different elements, but if you're going to display the menu on the food truck (which is highly recommended), don't change the staples and veer away from the main theme. The food presentation, names, ingredients, and the menu you have displayed on your truck should reflect your brand at all times. Quality and consistency help establish trust in your brand and create a group of loyal customers.

Design Attractive Packaging

Besides being delicious, the food you serve must be presented in attractive packaging — and not just to make it more appealing to customers. A spill-free, user-friendly packaging will tell your customers you care about their impression of food serving skills. Beyond this, by adding your brand's logo, tagline, and name to the packaging, you're prolonging that awareness and activating a recognition process that makes customers remember your brand and return to it. This is even more crucial if your concepts involve food delivery or catering services.

Make a Brand Book

After laying the foundation for your branding efforts, you can further build on it by making a brand book, which establishes essential guidelines for everyone involved in the business. The brand book not only includes its name but also its tagline, positioning strategy, voice and style, mission statement, logo design, fonts, colors, and other graphical elements, and how everyone representing the brand should interact with media channels (including social media). The contents of the brand book help everyone understand and make consistent efforts towards making a name for your business.

Extend Branding through Staff

Who better to embody a brand than its staff? Customers will more likely resonate with people who showcase the brand's values than with any catchy logo or design feature you choose to use during branding. The staff should carry the values you aim to represent with your menu and concept, as this is one of the best branding forms. For this, everyone should be on board with what the brand represents and incorporate it into their work — whether working directly with the customers or not. A uniform (even if it's a simple T-shirt with the food truck's logo on it) is a great addition to extended branding efforts.

Choosing the Right Equipment and Supplies

Now that you've mapped out where you'll place the equipment and know exactly what appliances and tools you can fit in your space, it's time to find the right ones. This can be as challenging as the design itself, but it doesn't have to be.

The first factor to consider is your concept, as this will determine the type of equipment you'll need to acquire. For example, buying a deep fryer is a must if one of your staples is crispy French fries. Likewise, if you serve grilled sandwiches or hamburgers, you'll most likely need a flat-top griddle. Your menu concept also plays a role in your refrigeration equipment choices. For instance, if you plan to cook from ingredients that require cold storage, you'll need to invest in high-quality refrigerators to keep the perishables safe to consume. If you are mostly using refrigerated ingredients, opt for a model with a built-in organizing space (this will make food prep easier).

When choosing the right equipment and supplies for your food truck, balance is key. You need to pick the right combination of what will fit and what will help you convert the space into a productive working area.

Quality is also fundamental, and not just for refrigeration. Even the pots, pans, and utensils will serve you better (and much longer) if they're high quality. They can transform basic chores into an effortless cooking experience. Moreover, investing in durable kitchen supplies and equipment will save you a considerable amount of money in the long run.

Consider investing in versatile cooking elements so you can use them for a variety of purposes, eliminating the need for additional equipment and space. Nowadays, customers value sustainable options, so investing in eco-friendly take-out boxes, cutlery, plates, serving bowls, and whatever else you might need based on your concept will be greatly appreciated.

Here are some cooking equipment options you might want to include in your food truck:

• **Microwave:** It can come in handy for heating various types of food.

• **Charbroiler:** Great for speeding up the cooking process and adding a bit more flavor to your food.

• **Fry Dump Station:** It keeps your fries warm and ready for the customers.

• **Soup Warme**r: It keeps soups hot throughout until served.

• **Cutting Boards:** Investing in a quality board will make slicing and dice easier.

- **Knives:** You'll need an assortment of knives to cut the different ingredients into the required shapes and sizes.

- **Food Thermometers:** These will help you ensure the food is thoroughly cooked and prevent food-borne illnesses.

- **Blenders:** They will come in handy when preparing smoothies and salsas.

- **Utensils:** To serve food to your customers. You can even use custom-made ones that align with your branding.

- **Customer Spice Shakers:** Your customers will appreciate having their own spice shaker to add more according to taste.

- **Disposable Gloves:** These are necessary for the hygienic handling of produce and preventing food-borne illnesses.

- **Food-Specific Refrigeration Appliances:** These will enable you to store everything at the optimal temperature. For example, you might want one refrigeration unit for the main food items and another one for fruit and other ingredients used for smoothies, beverages, etc.

- **Truck Cleaning Supplies:** Food trucks must be cleaned and disinfected daily, so it's good to have the essential supplies on hand. Beyond the hand sink, it's a good idea to invest in proper sanitizing chemicals, pressure washers, and trash bins.

- **Safety Equipment:** This is another must in a food truck. From fire extinguishers to first aid kits to smoke detectors, various elements need to be installed and maintained to ensure everyone's safety.

• **Personal Hygiene:** Don't forget about proper sanitation supplements and supplies either.

Chapter 6: Sourcing Ingredients and Menu Development

A great menu with quality and affordable items is central to the success of a food truck. Your ingredients will constantly need to be replenished as your supplies diminish with sales. Unlike a restaurant, for the most part, food trucks have a limited menu with only a few items on the list. Some trucks are known for the one specialty meal they sell. Therefore, crafting a great menu with quality ingredients will be a large contributor to defining your brand, adding to the spread of word-of-mouth marketing that is essential in any business today.

Depending on what you are making, there are a few options you need to consider when deciding on where you will source your ingredients. Your supplier choices will be based on price, ethics, and convenience. If the brand identity of your food truck includes sustainability, you would need to source goods locally to decrease your carbon footprint and ensure the farm or market you get your ingredients from runs an ethical operation regarding how they treat their animals and staff.

There is not a one-size-fits-all option when it comes to getting ingredients. Some food trucks may want the freshest and highest quality ingredients to create a high-end product, or you can just go to your local chain supermarket and get the cheapest options so you can keep your prices low and competitive. Therefore, what you cook, the location you are selling, and how much the items on your menu are will all contribute to the choice of your ingredients.

Before you decide where to purchase your ingredients from, you must craft an appropriate menu. Multiple factors go into developing your menu including your target market, your niche, your abilities, and the diets you are appealing to. It is essential to conduct thorough research on diet trends so your menu can seamlessly fit into the position you have carved out for your food truck.

Building Relationships with Suppliers

In business, your relationships are everything. When you have a strong bond with your supplier, you create more opportunities to get the best deals on ingredients. Furthermore, your supplier could do favors for you or will be the first to call you when they get new stock or have deals available. The types of suppliers you have will also determine what kind of relationship you can form. You probably have more bargaining power at a mom-and-pop store or a local farm than you would at a multinational warehouse chain.

A few options you can explore are wholesale food distributors, manufacturers, local suppliers, farmers' markets, food cooperatives, and shopping clubs. Each of these choices has unique pros and cons. Manufacturers require you to purchase in bulk most of the time. Any ingredient you get from a primary source will then be something that you use often and need a lot of. For example, a manufacturer supplier could be highly advantageous if your food truck sells dishes with potatoes as the base. However, the bulk buying that these kinds of suppliers require may not be advantageous to you if you do not use that much of the ingredient. Getting goods from a manufacturer could result in a lot of waste and overspending, so you must consider your needs carefully.

Using local or regional suppliers could also help you cut costs. If your supplier is in the area and serves the community you operate in, there is a higher chance that you will be able to negotiate better prices than if you stock from a huge multinational. You'll often find that regional suppliers have a higher appreciation for repeat customers than bigger brands because they are focused on a limited area.

Using local or regional suppliers could also help you cut costs. If your supplier is in the area and serves the community you operate in, there is a higher chance that you will be able to negotiate better prices than if you stock from a huge multinational. You'll often find that regional suppliers have a higher appreciation for repeat customers than bigger brands because they are focused on a limited area.

Farmer's markets are trending right now, but they can be a bit pricey. Furthermore, some sellers at farmer's markets can be disingenuous. It is common for some vendors to get their supplies from a wholesaler, and then repackage the products to give the impression that it is organic or local. You should do your due diligence in researching whether your farmers' market supplier is legitimate. Assuming that the supplier is not scamming, the benefit of shopping at a farmers' market is that it is a lot easier to build relationships and bargain. Using the fact that you source your ingredients from a farmers' market as part of your promotional brand identity appeals to a healthy and environmentally-conscious crowd. This could allow you to charge premium rates, effectively absorbing the additional cost it takes to shop at these kinds of markets.

Food cooperatives can help you save a lot of money. You can either join a cooperative that already exists, or you can approach food truck vendors and local restaurants to start one. Food cooperatives take advantage of bulk discounts by putting together funds so that they can buy items they all share. This requires you to form bonds with your competition to exploit this sourcing advantage. For a cooperative to work, you need to be sure that you are working with committed and reliable people.

Shopping clubs like BJ's Wholesale or Costco are a supply option that many restaurateurs make use of for their affordability. Although you pay a membership fee, the bulk discounts that you get make it well worth the cost. The disadvantage of using shopping clubs is that it is difficult to establish personal relationships, but if you repeatedly buy in high amounts from the same place, you could form relationships with managers that you can use to your benefit. For example, a supplier might call you first when new stock arrives, or they may allow you to buy with credit because they know you are a regular.

You must be loyal, consistent, and timely with payments so that a supplier knows that you are reliable. Your relationship with them can then become strong enough to allow you to ask for favors or discounts. If you fully embody your role as a reliable buyer, a supplier will be more open to helping you or charging you better prices. Friendliness also goes a long way. People are human at the end of the day, so if key players at your supplier like you as a person, they will be more open to helping you.

Creating a Unique and Profitable Menu

Due to menus being limited on a food truck, they are a cornerstone of your operation's identity. The first step to creating a menu is finding your niche. The boom in popularity of food trucks has saturated the market. Therefore, different lanes have been created. There is also the secondary and tertiary competition of restaurants, as well as convenience stores. Getting a niche people gravitate towards will help you target a segment of the market more easily. There are numerous ways to define a niche. First, you will need to define your target market according to your geographical area. Next, you must research what appeals to this market, as well as which trends are emerging. For example, spicy food has become a trend in the last few years, especially among younger people. Finally, you will analyze the competition you have and see what space you can fill. Many food trucks go for ethnic themes like Cuban, Mexican, or Italian food, but your niche does not necessarily have to fall into these boxes. You can give your food truck a 1950s diner feel or specialize in a specific meat type like chicken.

Once your niche has been determined, your menu will begin taking shape. There will probably already be people competing in your niche. If you are selling pizza, there is most likely another pizza store within a few miles from you. Developing a unique selling point is crucial. Put a spin on your niche that can make you stand out. Maybe it's a special sauce that only you have or some kind of signature pizza. You can also differentiate yourself by using novelty gimmicks. The atmosphere around your food truck is almost as important as the menu itself, so think deeply about how you can appeal to the public.

Homemade condiments can take your menu to the next level and could also open an additional income stream. You could serve your food with a special hot sauce, and if people like it, you can sell a bottled version. Condiments, sauces, and sides are a simple and cost-effective way to add variety to your menu. Research some recipes of condiments you will easily be able to prepare and calculate how much it will cost to serve. This will help you measure how much of the condiments you can provide for free or if you have to charge an additional cost for them. You can absorb the costs for your condiments into the price of your meals.

A common mistake beginners make is overcomplicating their menus. Offer a few streamlined options and some drink choices. This way, when you buy your supplies, it will be simpler, and people will know exactly what to expect from your food truck, making word-of-mouth promotion a lot easier. Five meal options, three sides, as well as a few beverages, are more than enough. Food trucks are a high-pressure environment where you are almost always aiming to get dishes out quickly. In these conditions, simplicity is your biggest ally.

Presentation is everything, especially in the age of social media. Nothing is better for a food truck than a viral meal. Make sure to take a lot of pictures and ask people to share their experiences at your food truck online. Novelty and gimmicks add to the virality of your food truck. Be brave, unique, and creative with your menu so that you give people something to talk about when they leave your sidewalk venue. Some food trucks are outpacing restaurants because of viral moments. Therefore, make sure that you form your menu in a way that considers the online environment. Don't think of yourself as a sidewalk salesman but rather as a food artist.

Lastly, when constructing your menu, you must consider which income bracket you are trying to appeal to. A middle-income food truck will not look the same as a higher-income one, and the area they are located in will also be vastly different. You must weigh the ingredients and supplies that you use against the prices of your foods, as well as decide which price point you want to use to appeal to a certain crowd. You can take the same pair of shoes and put them in Target and a designer store. If you ask people to guess how much the shoes cost, their perception of Target and a designer brand will make them state a price that varies greatly even though the product is the same. Nothing changed in terms of the materials, but the branding makes a world of difference. The prices on your menu are not simply about putting a markup on your costs, but they also communicate a message about your business, so they must align with your presentation.

Addressing Dietary Trends and Allergies

Fad diets come and go, but at their peak, they can make you a lot of money. Also, niche diets can create sustainability for your business in many ways. For example, a vegan food truck can appeal to both meat eaters and vegans. A food truck that has no vegan options, however, will lose an entire market segment. Understanding dietary trends will greatly impact how your business is structured.

A person's diet is influenced by numerous factors, including their health, religion, and culture. You cannot serve food that is too unfamiliar to people because no one would buy it. For example, in some Asian and African countries, it is not odd to serve insects as street food. If you were to serve that in a typical American city, you would probably not get many sales because the culture is not accustomed to that diet. However, trends could emerge where more people begin embracing that type of food, which could create a gap in the market. It is essential to know about various kinds of diets and food trends emerging in the market you aim to serve.

Sustainability and ethics have become increasingly impor-tant in the food industry in recent years. Consumers are becoming more aware of the process of getting their food to their table. As a food truck owner, you must analyze the market and determine how you can appeal to individuals who are not only looking for great-tasting food but are con-cerned about secondary factors like where your ingredients come from, if your menu is cruelty-free, and whether your offerings contain animal products.

In any business, you must have a plan and an understanding of the business cycle. First, your business will expand, then it will peak, and finally, it will either stagnate or fall. If you are appealing to fad diets, understand that they will rapidly grow and eventually fall. Your business model should then be planned around this reality so that it does not catch you by surprise. Once the fad dies, you will either need to rebrand your food truck or move on from the industry. When the fad is at its peak, you must be able to exploit it to its maximum potential.

Allergies are also a key consideration to make in the food industry because you could be held liable if you put someone's life at risk by unknowingly selling them a product that contains allergens. When you look at the ingredient list of any product on the shelf, they often issue a warning about the allergens the product contains to ensure the safety of the consumer. As a food truck owner, you must take the same precautions by either listing your ingredients or offering a similar warning. Some common food allergies include nuts, soy, dairy, and shellfish. If your food includes any of these ingredients, it is your responsibility to communicate that clearly to customers either verbally or with signage.

If you are selling food for a dietary segment, whether it is based on health, ethics, or religious beliefs, you must be honest. You cannot label something as paleo, keto, vegan, kosher, or halaal if the product does not meet those requirements. Firstly, this is a huge disservice to your patrons who trust you. They are the lifeblood of your business. Secondly, mislabeling your products can harshly bring down the hammer of the law if you are caught, so this dishonesty will also come at a huge risk to the sustainability of your business.

As someone in the food industry, you must keep an eye on dietary trends and allergies. The market for food trucks is constantly shifting. You will either have to adjust or watch your business fade away. The brilliance about owning a food truck is that the cost to rebrand is not as extensive as it would be if you owned a restaurant. Being able to evolve with the market is an underrated advantage in this industry.

Chapter 7: Marketing and Promotion

This chapter serves as a crash course on how to market and promote your food truck. You'll learn how to define your target audience, build a favorable brand image, and set achievable marketing goals. You'll also find out how to create effective social media strategies, establish a strong online presence, and leverage the available online tools to increase your brand awareness and reach a wider target audience.

Build a Target Persona

Your marketing plan is deeply tied to all the steps mentioned in the previous chapter. It requires you to have a solid understanding of your niche and USPs. You should also integrate it into your budget and financial planning. Creating a target persona is key when it comes to deciding the marketing channels, vehicles, and objectives, as well as your creative strategy.

Your target persona is your ideal customer. For instance, when most people hear the term "food truck," they might imagine a 25-year-old woman who lives in an urban area and has an office job or works as a freelancer. She enjoys exploring unique and diverse culinary experiences but leans toward healthy options and is active on social media platforms, especially Instagram. She's middle- to upper-class and always seeks a balance between quality and affordability. She values sustainability, prefers to support eco-friendly businesses, and enjoys social gatherings and outdoor activities. She relies on Instagram and TikTok to discover new food options and hangout spots and leads a busy lifestyle that leaves her with little time to prepare her food. She is constantly on the hunt for convenient, quick, and satisfying culinary experiences.

Keep in mind that your target persona might differ depending on what your USPs are. For instance, if your food truck is more innovative and is targeting an unusual segment, such as children (and their guardians) or athletes who are seeking convenient food options with high protein and low-calorie content, then your target will change entirely. Knowing your target persona is essential if you want to know where to find and how to reach your audience.

Set Your Marketing Goals

After you've determined your target persona, you need to set marketing goals. Increasing brand awareness, generating leads, increasing revenue, retaining customers, increasing conversion rates, and acquiring customers are among the most popular marketing goals. Since you'll be introducing your food truck business to your target audience for the first time, your primary marketing goal should be to increase your brand awareness. While most businesses' primary goal is to increase revenues, you can't make sales and earn profits if people don't know about your business.

Brand Identity and Positioning

Having a strong brand identity and a favorable position in consumers' minds is crucial for the performance of your business. Those two elements are among the leading factors in how consumers relate to your brand, perceive it, and trust it. Your brand's positioning and identity are key tools when it comes to increasing awareness and boosting memorability and brand recognition.

They allow consumers to view you as a fit competitor in your industry so they can start comparing you with them in terms of preference and value. Not only do they boost recognition, but how you maintain your identity and position can either hinder or foster consumer loyalty. When consumers are loyal to your brand, they become emotionally attached to it, making them less likely to switch to a competitor and more likely to recommend you to others.

Brand Identity

Brand identity is everything that sets you apart from all others in the market. It is the emotions tied to the brand, its name, logo, visuals, color scheme, fonts, verbal and written messages, and the way you (or your employees) communicate and interact with others on behalf of the brand. The brand's identity is the key to leaving a consistent, and therefore recognizable, impression on your target audience.

Sure, having an eye-catching logo and a memorable tagline is great. However, this is not enough to successfully build and maintain a memorable brand image. You stand out by being authentic and representing your brand's values in everything you do. Brand identity is the feelings you instigate and the holistic experience you offer to your customers. Innovation, growth, and evolution are needed. However, you should always keep in touch with your brand's roots. A brand identity isn't a temporary marketing or business strategy. Basically, it's who your brand would be if it were a person.

Your brand identity is based on your vision, mission, purpose, values, target persona, and brand personality. Once you have these aspects set in stone, you can start working on the visual elements. What you communicate to the world should embody this identity.

Brand Positioning

Brand positioning is the strategy you use to create a desirable position for your brand in your target audience's minds. For example, when considering different car brands, you might automatically find yourself comparing them based on price and quality. Your perception of each brand is ingrained in your mind- this is known as brand positioning. For instance, you might naturally place Mercedes (high price, high quality) in a more desirable position, in terms of quality, than Kia (lower price, lower quality).

How you want to position yourself depends on your value proposition. If, for example, your USPs are convenient and high-quality meals, you'll position yourself positively on that spectrum. If you're focusing on offering healthy and affordable meals, then this is how you'll position yourself in the minds of consumers.

To put yourself in the desirable position, you need to focus heavily on communicating your value proposition and competitive advantage. Most of your communication messages should highlight how your brand solves a certain problem or addresses an unfulfilled need that your target market has. You've successfully positioned your brand if your target audience aligns the products you offer with the time, place, need, and what you intend. For instance, a protein bar brand will want its target audience to align it with the time before, during, or after workouts, the gym (or the location of the sport they play), the need for a high-protein snack, and the want for convenience and affordability. When all of these aspects are instigated, the well-positioned brand will be considered by the consumer.

Social Media and Online Presence

Your target audience and market research will help you determine which platforms you'll find your target customers on. Generally, however, if you're targeting a younger demographic, you should focus most of your online marketing efforts on Instagram, TikTok, and Google. It doesn't matter which platforms you're using as long as they allow you to reach and interact with your target audience effectively; you maintain a consistent brand identity, you deliver the same messages across all platforms, and you maintain a consistent posting schedule on all of them.

Instagram

Leverage Instagram's visual nature for storytelling. Only share appetizing and high-quality images of your food. The success of your online presence depends on your ability to create visually appealing content. You should also make an effort to diversify your content. A good way to ensure that there's content variety is to categorize your posts into convincing, inspiring, educating, and engaging/entertaining content.

• *Content Strategy*

Convincing posts are the ones that include a direct CTA (call to action). These posts might tell you where to find the brand, what your USPs and value propositions are, why consumers should choose you over your competitors, and share news about offers, deals, and promotions. Inspiring content is a more indirect way of selling your products. It relies on sharing positive reviews and feedback, success stories, blog posts and PR, influencer or celebrity collaborations, live content, and high-quality images of what you offer to inspire your target audience to purchase your products.

Educational posts are shareable and valuable relevant tips that you can offer to your consumers. These can also include fun facts about the general product category you're offering or the industry you're operating in. An Italian restaurant can create a post about the history of pasta (as long as they keep it fun, short, and light) or the most popular type of pasta in the world. Entertaining posts are the ones that encourage your target audience to engage with your brand through answering questions, polls, quizzes, tagging people in the comments section, or other online activations. The Italian restaurant might share a post with the headline "What your favorite type of pasta says about you."

The percentage that creators allocate to each content category differs based on their strategy and marketing goals. However, as a rule of thumb, it's best to prioritize your content accordingly: inspirational (highest priority), convincing, engaging, and informative (lowest priority).

• *Content Calendar*

Preparing content is not always easy and can be time-consuming. Preparing a monthly content calendar allows you to stay active on social media and maintain a consistent posting schedule, especially when you already have so much on your plate. There are several social media tools available online that you can use to determine the best days and times to post, depending on your location and target audience's demographics.

Determine the best 4 days in the week to post and the time at which your target users are the most active on each day. At the start of each month, you'll prepare the visual and text material for the 16 posts you'll need for the month. In addition to your posts, try to stay active on your Instagram stories, especially on the days you won't be posting. You'll find free content calendar templates online that will allow you to neatly organize your monthly content into the following categories: day, visuals, time, platform, key messaging, captions, hashtags, and more.

• *Feed, Stories, Engagement, and Reels*

Your posts will be organized into a grid pattern on your Instagram feed. When someone checks out your account, you want to make sure that your grid looks appealing and aesthetically pleasing. You also want it to convey your brand image and illicit the correct thoughts and feelings. You want people to understand what you're selling and why you stand out just by scrolling through your grid.

Use a cohesive, branded color scheme and fonts across your posts. If you're posting reels, you can create covers for them so that their appearance on the grid aligns with your general aesthetic strategy. You can browse through Pinterest or other Instagram profiles for inspiration. When you're not posting, the best way to retain engagement is through stories. You can use Instagram stories to show behind-the-scenes moments, daily specials, and event preparations. They're also a great way to interact with your audience through polls, quizzes, and Q&A boxes. Reels are great for expanding your reach. Use them to create short, engaging, and creative videos to showcase your food, staff, people enjoying your food, and the general vibe of your food truck.

Engage with your customers consistently by promptly responding to their comments and direct messages. Use your stories, captions, and offline marketing tools, such as banners and posters, to encourage them to share their experiences at your food truck. Ask them to tag you in their stories or even send you direct messages with feedback, images, and videos of them having a great time at your truck.

The best way to boost consumer loyalty and garner emotional attachment is by creating a customer-centric online and offline experience and engaging them in your overall strategy. You can also create a unique, easy, and memorable branded hashtag for your food truck, encouraging users to use it whenever they post about you. Use your branded hashtag, along with other trending and local hashtags (specialized online tools can help you determine the best hashtags to use based on your industry, target audience, marketing goals, and location), to expand your reach.

• *Collaborations, Promotions, and Contests*

Partner with local influencers to reach a broader audience. Choose individuals with a favorable image who are relevant to your industry or would generally benefit from your USP. If you're offering delicious food in general, you can target a food blogger. If you're offering healthy food options, you can target both food bloggers and wellness influencers (this will help you emphasize the fact that your food is both healthy and delicious). Influencers can create engaging content featuring or reviewing your food, inspiring their own follower base to try your food.

Think of other creative ways to cross-promote your product with other players in the industry. For instance, a protein bar brand might partner with gyms to cross-promote both brands. The brand might place stands in partner gyms featuring the product. This way, anyone who goes there to work out might feel compelled to try it out. In exchange, the protein bar brand can create stories and posts with a "find us at ... gym." The gym and the protein bar brand can create a cross-promotional campaign where anyone who posts a picture eating the protein bar under a certain hashtag can receive 10% off at the gym. Both brands can post reels showcasing people working out at the gym and having the protein bar as a mid-workout snack. The possibilities are endless.

• *Promotions and Contests*

You can encourage people to visit your truck by creating limited-time offers and discounts and promoting them on your social media. You can also host contests and give-aways, encouraging followers to share your posts or tag their friends in the comments section for a chance to win a free meal. You can cross-promote your promotions and contests with your chosen influencers for a wider reach and higher engagement.

TikTok

Your TikTok account should maintain the same brand identity and key messaging as your Instagram account. One of the greatest advantages of TikTok is that it offers a higher chance of virality and allows you to reach a wider audience. Use the app to create short-form, engaging, and highly entertaining content. You want to capture your audience's attention within the first few seconds.

• *Trending and Diverse Content*

Hop on trending challenges and think of ways in which you can join them creatively. This is one of the best ways in which you can increase your visibility. Make sure, however, to only hop on trends that align with your brand image, personality, and values. If your food truck is characterized by its fun, light-hearted, cheerful, and energetic spirit, there is no harm in showcasing your team participating in a viral TikTok dance or challenge in front of your food truck.

Use trending sounds, transitions, and video shooting techniques to show behind-the-scenes moments, your food, and the atmosphere at your food truck. You can also create educational content on TikTok, where you share short videos to educate your audience about your industry or cuisine, offer cooking tips, or discuss cooking and food presentation techniques.

• *Collaborations, Engagement, and Duets*

Like Instagram, you can collaborate with popular TikTok creators who are relevant to your industry and can benefit from your products so they can feature your truck in their videos. Use the captions in your TikTok to boost engagement by encouraging your target audience to duet your videos, use your brand-specific hashtag, and reply in the comments.

You can also use the in-app polls and Q&A features to drive interactions and engagement with users. Maintain a consistent posting schedule on TikTok (3-4 times a week) and use specialized tools to determine the best hashtags to use and times to post. Aside from virality, you want to use TikTok to communicate your brand's personality to users. It is a way to create a memorable brand image, build anticipation, and create an emotional connection with your target audience.

Google

While a website can be an added value to your brand and can serve as a supplementary platform that offers additional resources and information to customers, you don't really need it. You might want to consider including it in your expansion plan if you're going to sell branded items or ingredients further down the line, allowing customers to order online. For now, you can benefit from Google's promotional services without a website.

Google Business (formerly known as Google My Business (GMP)) is an invaluable tool for businesses because it allows them to manage their online presence on the search engine. You can provide information regarding your offerings, business hours, customer reviews, contact details, location, and appearance on Google Maps through this tool. You can also target ads on Google, so your social media accounts and Google Business listing appear in search results. Practice search engine optimization (SEO) by integrating keywords into your listing and content across social media accounts.

You're now ready to introduce your business to the world. Remember to continuously analyze your performance on all your online platforms by observing engagement, analytics, and conversions. Refine and adjust your strategy based on your performance and audience feedback. Consistency, creativity, and staying true to your brand's identity are key to your marketing and promotional success.

Chapter 8: Operations and Management

In the food truck industry, operations and management are the heart and soul of the business. These processes include everything from handling day-to-day stuff like cooking and serving to managing each process for effective workflow.

Proper operations and management in your food truck bring a lot of good. First off, it makes everything run like a well-oiled machine, making sure customers have a great experience from ordering to munching down. It's all about providing good service and using resources wisely so you don't spend too much money and can make a good profit.

In a world where food options are everywhere, a food truck with top-notch operations and management stands out. It keeps customers coming back for more tasty meals. The aim here is to create a strong and customer-friendly business that can handle the twists and turns of the food truck industry.

Staffing and Training

Staffing and training are crucial aspects of running a successful food truck business. In the food industry, customer satisfaction is often directly linked to the quality of service and the food itself. Here's a breakdown of staffing and training considerations for a food truck business.

Staffing

Chef/Cook

The chef or cook is the anchor of the food truck. Their responsibilities extend beyond merely preparing and cooking the menu items. They must also manage the entire cooking process within the confined space of the truck. This demands a deep understanding of various cooking techniques, flavor combinations, and the ability to adapt recipes to fit the limited space. Time management skills are critical, especially during peak hours, to ensure that orders are not only perfect but also served promptly.

Service Staff

The service staff serves as the direct interface between the food truck and its customers. Their role involves not just taking orders and processing transactions but also managing customer inquiries and feedback. Effective customer service skills are paramount, encompassing clear communication, patience, and the ability to handle potentially challenging customer interactions with professionalism. Additionally, proficiency in cash handling is crucial to maintaining the accuracy and integrity of transactions.

Driver

The driver holds a unique position in the food truck business, as they are responsible for the physical mobility of the entire operation. Beyond possessing a valid driver's license, the driver must be well-versed in local traffic laws, possess navigation skills, and ensure the regular maintenance of the vehicle. Reliability is a key attribute, as timely arrival at scheduled locations is crucial for the success of the business.

Assistant/Helper

Assistants or helpers provide crucial support across various operational facets of the food truck. Their tasks may include assisting with food preparation, maintaining cleanliness, and handling organizational responsibilities. Adaptability is a central skill for this role, given the dynamic nature of tasks in a fast-paced environment. A willingness to learn and physical stamina are equally important qualities to navigate the diverse demands of the role.

Training

Food Safety and Handling
Comprehensive training in food safety and handling is imperative to uphold health standards. Staff must be well-versed in proper food storage practices, hygiene protocols, and measures to prevent cross-contamination. This training ensures that the food served maintains the highest quality and safety standards.

Customer Service
Customer service training goes beyond the basics of order-taking. It includes effective communication, understanding customer preferences, and resolving issues with finesse. The focus is on creating a positive and memorable customer experience, as customer satisfaction is often a key determinant of the food truck's success.

Menu Knowledge
Staff training includes an in-depth understanding of the menu, covering not only the ingredients but also allergens and preparation methods. This knowledge empowers staff to provide accurate information to customers, fostering transparency and trust.

Efficient Workflow
Efficient workflow training addresses the unique challenges of working within the confined space of a food truck. Time management skills are honed to ensure a streamlined

process, from order receipt to food preparation and service. This is particularly crucial during busy periods to prevent bottlenecks and delays.

Cash Handling

Proper cash handling training is fundamental. Staff must be proficient in counting money, giving back accurate change, and operating any point-of-sale systems in use. This not only safeguards against errors but also contributes to the overall trustworthiness of the business.

Equipment Operation

Given the reliance on specialized equipment within a food truck, staff training covers the operation and maintenance of all tools and appliances. This includes a deep understanding of cooking equipment, cleaning tools, and any technological systems used for transactions.

Health and Safety

Health and safety training is extensive, encompassing emergency procedures, fire safety, and the correct handling of cleaning chemicals. This knowledge ensures a secure working environment for all staff, mitigating potential risks and hazards.

Crisis Management

Staff are trained to handle unexpected challenges, such as equipment malfunctions or shortages of key ingredients. This training focuses on problem-solving skills, quick decision-making, and maintaining composure under pressure to mitigate any disruptions to the operational flow.

Local Regulations

Thorough understanding and adherence to local health and safety regulations, as well as obtaining the necessary permits and licenses, are critical aspects of staff training. Compliance guarantees that the food truck operates within the legal framework, avoiding potential legal issues.

Team Building

Team building exercises and communication skills development are integral to fostering a positive team environment. A cohesive and supportive team enhances collaboration, ensuring that the entire staff works together seamlessly, even during the most demanding periods.

The staffing and training aspects of a food truck business require meticulous attention to detail. By honing the skills of each staff member and providing comprehensive training, a food truck can not only deliver exceptional food but also create a positive and efficient customer experience.

Efficient Workflow and Time Management

Efficient workflow and time management are critical elements in the success of a food truck business, where a streamlined process is essential to meet customer demands, maintain quality, and maximize operational efficiency.

Efficient Workflow
Order Reception
• *Streamlined Point of Sale (POS):* Invest in a Point of Sale system that not only automates the order-taking process but

is also user-friendly. A streamlined POS minimizes the time spent on transactional activities, reducing the likelihood of errors and enhancing overall efficiency.

• *Clear Communication Channels:* Establish a clear and efficient communication system between the service staff and the kitchen. This can involve the use of technology such as order management software or designated communication areas within the food truck. The aim is to facilitate the prompt transmission of orders, minimizing delays in food preparation.

Food Preparation

• *Prep List and Organization:* Develop a comprehensive prep list for each shift, outlining all the necessary ingredients and tasks required for efficient food preparation. Organize the workspace in a way that minimizes unnecessary movement and optimally utilizes the limited space available in a food truck.

• *Batch Cooking:* Plan the menu and cooking processes to allow for batch cooking of certain items. This approach not only reduces the overall cooking time but also ensures a consistent flow during peak hours, as popular items can be partially prepared in advance.

Assembly Line Approach

• *Task Delegation:* Assign specific tasks to each team member based on their skills and expertise. This could include dividing responsibilities such as chopping, grilling, assembling, and packaging. By clearly defining roles, the workflow becomes more structured and streamlined.

• *Sequential Order:* Organize the workflow in a sequential order that mirrors the natural progression of preparing and assembling dishes. This sequential approach minimizes bottlenecks and ensures a smooth flow from ingredient preparation to the final stages of cooking and assembly.

Service and Delivery

• *Order Timing:* Coordinate the timing of food preparation with customer orders. Analyze historical data to predict peak hours and adjust the preparation accordingly. Having popular items partially prepared during slower periods can expedite service during peak hours.

• *Efficient Service Windows:* Design the layout of the food truck with an emphasis on optimizing service windows. Make sure that both staff and customers can easily access the service areas, reducing congestion and facilitating a more efficient service process.

Time Management
Shift Planning
• *Rotations and Breaks:* Develop a meticulous shift schedule that takes into account the need for staff rotations and breaks. Avoiding staff burnout is crucial for maintaining productivity throughout the day.

• *Pre-Shift Meetings:* Conduct brief pre-shift meetings to outline priorities, menu changes, and any special considerations for the day. This ensures that all staff members are on the same page and aware of any adjustments to the workflow.

Inventory Management
• *Regular Inventory Checks:* Implement a systematic approach to regular inventory checks. This proactive measure helps in identifying and addressing potential shortages before they become critical, minimizing disruptions during service.

• *Supplier Coordination*: Work closely with suppliers to coordinate delivery schedules. By aligning deliveries with operational needs, you can optimize the supply chain and reduce the risk of running out of key ingredients.

Adaptability and Problem-solving
• *Staff Training:* Provide thorough training to staff members on problem-solving skills and adaptability. Cross-train employees to perform multiple roles so that the team can seamlessly adapt to changing demands or unexpected challenges.

• **Contingency Plans:** Develop comprehensive contingency plans for potential disruptions, such as equipment malfunctions, shortages of ingredients, or changes in location. Having well-thought-out plans in place enables the team to react swiftly and effectively to unexpected situations.

Data Analysis

• **Performance Analytics:** Utilize data analytics tools to analyze performance metrics. This can include peak hours, popular menu items, and customer preferences. By leveraging this data, you can make informed decisions to optimize workflow during specific timeframes.

• **Feedback Loops:** Establish robust feedback loops with staff members. Encourage open communication and gather insights on areas that could be streamlined or improved. Regular feedback sessions can also contribute to a continuous improvement mindset within the team.

Technology Integration

• **Mobile Ordering:** Consider integrating mobile ordering apps into your operations. These apps allow customers to place orders in advance, reducing on-site wait times and allowing the team to manage order flow more effectively during peak hours.

• **Automated Systems**: Implement automated systems wherever feasible. This could include order tracking systems that reduce manual errors and enhance the overall efficiency of the order fulfillment process.

Efficient workflow and time management in a food truck business requires meticulous attention to detail across various operational aspects. By strategically organizing tasks, optimizing processes, fostering a culture of adaptability, and utilizing technology, a food truck can achieve heightened levels of both customer satisfaction and overall operational success.

Inventory Control and Supply Chain Management

Inventory Control
• *Inventory Tracking Systems*

Implement an inventory tracking system that provides real-time visibility into stock levels. This system can utilize barcoding, RFID technology, or specialized inventory management software. Barcoding allows for accurate and efficient scanning of items, while RFID technology enables automatic tracking of inventory movement.

• *Categorization and Organization*

Categorize inventory items based on various factors, such as perishability, popularity, and frequency of use. Establish a systematic organization within the storage space of the food truck, employing techniques like ABC analysis to prioritize high-value items and ensure easy access during busy periods.

• Regular Audits and Counts
Conduct frequent physical audits and counts of the inventory to maintain accuracy. This involves comparing physical stock levels against digital records. Implement a systematic schedule for these audits, ensuring that discrepancies are promptly identified and rectified.

• First-in-First-Out (FIFO) Method
Follow the First-In-First-Out method. That ensures that the oldest inventory is used or sold first, minimizing the risk of food spoilage and waste. The inventory system should automatically track expiration dates to facilitate this process.

• Threshold Alerts
Set up threshold alerts within the inventory management system to notify staff when certain items reach predefined minimum levels. This feature enhances proactive management, allowing for timely reordering before items run out, thereby preventing stockouts.

• Supplier Collaboration
Establish a collaborative relationship with suppliers. This involves regular communication to convey expectations, negotiate favorable terms, and address any issues promptly. Collaborative supplier relationships can lead to more flexible arrangements, such as just-in-time delivery, reducing the need for excessive on-site storage.

• Menu Analysis
Conduct rigorous analyses of sales data and customer preferences to make informed decisions about the menu. Regularly review the performance of each item and adjust

the menu accordingly. This iterative process ensures that the inventory is aligned with customer demand, preventing overstocking of slow-moving items.

Supply Chain Management
• Supplier Relationships
Develop and nurture strong relationships with suppliers. Transparent communication is essential for understanding their capabilities and constraints. Negotiate mutually beneficial terms, including payment schedules, bulk discounts, and consistent quality standards.

• Multiple Suppliers
Diversify the supplier base to mitigate risks associated with reliance on a single source. Having multiple suppliers for critical items provides flexibility, reduces vulnerability to disruptions, and allows for strategic negotiations based on market conditions.

• Lead Time Management
Understand the lead times associated with each supplier. This involves analyzing historical data to determine the time between order placement and actual delivery. Accurate lead time
management is crucial for avoiding stockouts and optimizing inventory levels.

• Forecasting and Demand Planning
Leverage historical sales data, market trends, and customer preferences for accurate demand forecasting. Implement demand planning techniques to optimize inventory levels

and ordering quantities. This involves using statistical models, machine learning algorithms, or industry benchmarks to predict future demand patterns.

• Temperature Control for Perishables

Implement stringent temperature control measures, especially for perishable items. Regularly monitor and maintain optimal storage conditions during transportation and within the food truck. Use technology such as temperature sensors and monitoring systems to stay compliant with food safety standards.

• Contingency Planning

Develop comprehensive contingency plans for potential disruptions in the supply chain. This involves identifying alternative suppliers, creating emergency stockpiles of critical items, and having well-defined protocols for addressing unexpected challenges, such as natural disasters or sudden market fluctuations.

• Technology Integration

Integrate technology into supply chain management processes for enhanced efficiency. Utilize order processing software, track deliveries in real-time, and leverage data analytics to optimize the supply chain. Automation can streamline routine tasks, minimize errors, and provide valuable insights for strategic decision-making.

• Sustainability Considerations

Incorporate sustainability considerations into supply chain decisions. This involves sourcing ingredients responsibly, minimizing waste through sustainable packaging, and supporting suppliers with eco-friendly practices. Aligning the supply chain with sustainability goals contributes to environmental responsibility and meets the expectations of environmentally conscious consumers.

• *Quality Assurance*

Implement rigorous quality assurance measures throughout the supply chain. This includes inspecting incoming shipments, verifying the quality of ingredients, and ensuring that suppliers
adhere to agreed-upon quality standards. Regular audits and inspections contribute to maintaining the highest quality standards for the food truck's offerings.

• *Continuous Improvement*

Foster a culture of continuous improvement within the supply chain. Regularly review processes, gather feedback from staff, suppliers, and customers, and implement enhancements to streamline operations and enhance overall efficiency. This iterative approach ensures that the supply chain evolves to meet the evolving needs of the business.

Meticulous attention to detail in both inventory control and supply chain management is paramount for the success of a food truck business. The integration of advanced technologies, strategic supplier relationships, and a commitment to sustainability contributes to an optimized and resilient operational framework. Through these measures, a food truck can deliver high-quality products efficiently, meeting customer expectations while managing costs effectively.

Chapter 9: Location and Events

Food truck owners don't usually think about locations. Many park anywhere that catches their fancy, see if their business is making a profit, and move on to try another spot. It may seem like a good strategy, but it's not efficient. In the long, you tend to waste a lot of time, effort, and fuel just to find the right spot. Careful planning is the key.

Choosing Profitable Locations

Food trucks aren't anything new. They have been doing great business since the early 1900s, but not all of them. A major difference between a successful food truck and an unsuccessful one is the location. Two hot dog stands of the same brand in different parts of the city don't do equally well, and that is only because of the location. Here are a few great tips to help you choose a profitable location for your food truck.

• *Picking the Right City*
There are cities that will grant you a food truck permit for a reasonable cost in a short time, like Philadelphia, and Indianapolis. Then there are cities like Boston and San Francisco, where you need to go through several procedures, make a number of trips to government institutions, and pay exorbitant fees before you can acquire a permit. Which location would you choose? The ones with reasonable costs and short times for permits, right?

The thing is, other food truck owners are most probably thinking along the same lines. You may find more competition in Philadelphia or Denver than in Boston or San Francisco. Consider the extra time, effort, and money spent in acquiring a permit as an investment that may bear fruit soon after you launch your food truck business in a less competitive environment.

• *Parking Permissions*
The next step is finding the right spot. Ideally, any given place in the city can be your parking spot, so start with the

process of elimination. Strike out the places on the map where you know you won't get parking permissions. If there is a restaurant in the vicinity, you may not be able to park there. The same goes for schools or government buildings.

• *Foot Traffic*

Most of your business will come from marketing campaigns and promotional ventures, but a substantial part of it may also be from the foot traffic in the area. Oftentimes, people don't decide beforehand to have a meal at a food truck. Quite a few notice the place while going about their day and find themselves eating there on a whim. The more foot traffic in the area, the greater the likelihood of something like that to happen.

You can check the foot traffic in different sections of the city at a government or a private institution that monitors such things. You can decide your food truck location based on the data. If they aren't willing to part with the data, check the foot traffic yourself by sitting at your shortlisted locations during peak hours for a few days.

• *Target Audience*

Studies show that middle-class, middle-aged people tend to frequent food trucks the most. So, don't park your truck at a high-end location, thinking that you can raise your prices and make more profit. The number of customers there may not even cover your expenses.

Additionally, the kind of food you are serving may not be pre-ferred by the foot traffic of your parking spot. Selling frozen desserts near corporate high-rises may not be as profitable as parking before a kids' play area. Check if your chosen spot has the demographic that best aligns with your business.

• **_Customer Parking_**

Parking in a crowded place doesn't necessarily mean getting more customers. One of the main reasons is customer parking. If someone wants to eat at your food truck but cannot find a good parking space nearby, they will simply drive away. Pick a location where you can park your truck comfortably, and so can your customers. Make sure there is enough space around the truck for parking at least two cars.

• **_Location Ideas_**

You haven't found the right spot yet or don't know where to start? Here are a few first-rate location ideas for you to start exploring.

1. Food Truck Park: These days, the most obvious choice for a food truck is a dedicated park. You will save a ton of money on marketing efforts because the park owners may conduct their own promotions, and seeing a bright variety of food trucks and smelling a myriad of food flavors all in one place will automatically reel in potential customers off the street. You only need to find a park without a similar food truck to avoid sharing potential customers.

2. At/Near Office Premises: Most of your target demographic works in some kind of office (private or governmental). Pick any towering office building that will likely have thousands of employees and apply for permission to park on the curb nearby. Better yet, find a spot in sight of multiple buildings. Parking outside hospitals is also a great option to feed the family and friends of patients.

3. At/Near College Campuses: College students eat the same kind of food due to budget and time constraints. Many of them crave something different. Help them satiate their cravings by parking somewhere near campus. You will have hit it big if you are able to secure permission to park near or on campus.

4. In Residential Areas or Suburbs: In residential areas, there isn't much foot traffic, but you have a chance to develop a regular, permanent customer base. Permissions are hard to get, but approach the local apartment or suburb association and try your luck. You won't get permanent parking, however. The best you can do is get a temporary parking space for a set time during which customers usually eat the kind of food you cook.

5. Near Construction Sites: Construction workers usually bring their lunch boxes, but a few hours of hard work after lunch may leave them starving again. That is when they will line up outside your truck for a quick bite.

6. Around Gas Stations: Gas stations have plenty of parking space and a regular stream of customers. Look for a station that doesn't offer cooked food in the attached store to avoid conflicts with the manager.

Participating in Events and Festivals

Events and festivals are a great way to promote your food truck business and build your brand in the industry. There are festivals specifically organized for food trucks. Many other non-food-related events also call for food trucks to cater to the attendees. If you haven't set your stall up in an event before, here are a few easy steps you can follow.

1. Find the Right Festival

You can't expect to sell your meat-filled tacos or cheeseburgers at a vegan festival. Look for the right kind of festival to sell your food. If you offer both meat and vegan cuisine, you may need to tweak your menu depending on the type of event. Go through the website of the festival and look for the type of food usually served. If it's an annual event, check out which food trucks had parked there the previous year. You can't find much information on their website? Contact the organizers directly and ask if they are accepting food vendors like you at the event.

2. Send Your Application

Event organizers won't simply accept you as a vendor based on a brief phone call. You will need to submit a formal application to show your interest in the event. Ask them how to send an application and what details and papers should be enclosed. If they have one, browse through the application section of their website. You will most likely have to approach the organizer in person to fill out the relevant application form.

Don't be too boastful in your application or use colorful language. Be clear and concise, and state your hygiene and cleanliness standards. Highlight the items your customers love the most. References and recommendations are also appreciated.

3. Book the Right Spot

The right food truck spot at a festival can go a long way to help you make profits. After all, they are temporary events, and people may not have time to explore the entire line of offerings. You don't want to be in some remote corner of the event where the lighting is low, and it smells bad. You also don't want to be right where the entrance is. Rarely anyone starts eating immediately after entering the festival.

Pick a spot somewhere in the middle, in the thick of the action. If it is a music concert, make sure you are far enough from the headbanging crowd but well in sight of them. At business events, you want to be near the edge of the seating lineup, within reach of the bordering seats.

4. Gathering the Essentials

Once you have fixed everything else, it's time to gather the essentials and decorate your food truck to attract the on-coming crowd at the event. Make sure you have all the ingredients at hand and then some. You don't want to keep your customers waiting as you head out to buy more ingredients.

Recreate your menu to suit the kind of festival you're serving at. For instance, at a rock concert, you want to stock ready-to-serve food like sandwiches and snacks because the audience wants to get back into things after having a quick bite.

If the event is happening outside your city, you will need a valid food license from the health department in that region. A separate, temporary vendor's permit may also be required. Check with the local authorities well beforehand. Additionally, food truck insurance is recommended while setting up outside your operating area.

Breaking into Food Trucks Catering for Regional Catering Events

If you have a thriving food truck business and wish to carve a path into the profitable world of catering, know that all your official work is already done. You can apply for a separate catering license to look even more professional, but it is not required. Your food truck licenses are usually enough. All you need now is a bit of experience to get the ball rolling. Here are a few excellent tips to help you on your way to becoming a reputable food truck caterer.

• **Reach Out to Your Regular Customers**
They are your regular customers for a reason. They keep coming back because they like your food. Let them know that you are available for catering purposes. Ask them to call you if they are organizing a party or an event. Make them aware that you are open to suggestions on expanding your menu. If they seem interested, show them your strategy to make their event successful, at least from the catering viewpoint.

• Leverage Your Food Truck Marketing Channels

Reuse all the channels you had used for marketing your food truck, but this time, for your catering business. Add the catering option and highlight it in your marketing flyers, emails, banners, etc. Let your social media followers know about your new venture via posts and stories. In short, you don't need to completely transform your business marketing strategy. Just add another avenue and keep it running smoothly.

• Start Off Small

You don't have to look for a major opportunity right off the bat. Start with a birthday party in the family or a friend's bachelorette. Pick something you can manage with one or two staff members. One catering experience in your resume, no matter how small, can do wonders for landing your next gig. That said, if you manage to bag a major event, don't shy away. Accept the invitation and execute the catering to the best of your ability.

• Hire Employees and Delegate

You may be able to manage your food truck all on your own or with another cook or cashier. However, for a catering business, you will need more than just two or three people. You will need at least one each of a cook, server, host, kitchen helper, and supervisor. You may also need cleaners after closing.

Once you have hired the necessary staff, trust in their capabilities. Don't try to do all the work on your own. Delegate the less important stuff to the supervisor or manager and let them handle the rest of the staff. Your main job as the owner is to make sure that everything runs smoothly and to resolve any conflicts that may arise.

• Understand the Client's Requirements

Most catering businesses fail because they don't meet their client's requirements and expectations. So far, you ran the food truck on your own terms. While transitioning into catering, you should learn to organize the event on their terms. Do they want their offerings arranged a certain way? How much ready food do they wish to display on the counter? How spicy should it be? Do they want to include a mini-bar too?

Ideally, the client would state their requirements before hiring you. In an effort to cover all bases, ask them every little question regarding catering that comes to mind. Let them know that it's your first event and apologize for any inconvenience, but assure them that it will benefit their event first before it does your business.

Chapter 10: Technology and Innovation

Did you know there are more than 40,000 food trucks operating in the US? They don't just compete amongst themselves but against restaurants too (which are in excess of

700,000). Don't be just a part of this growing industry. Show your customers that you are spearheading growth with innovative solutions that will propel your business miles ahead of the rest. Incorporate the following technologies into your food truck to stand apart from your competition.

Implementing Point of Sale (POS) Systems

A point of sale (POS) is a point in a business when the customer completes the transaction by making the payment. In food trucks, when they hand you the cash and you give them the receipt and the food, that is a POS. There was a time when business owners used to keep a tally of such transactions on a piece of paper. Cash registers made it more efficient, but the revolutionary transaction technology available today has transformed the nature of POS systems.

• Taking orders has become faster than ever. Your cook will be notified of the order immediately after you add it to the system. It is especially beneficial during peak hours when you have to service long queues that are getting longer still. A POS system brings down the waiting time to a bare minimum.

• The technology doesn't take up much space, making it doubly important for a mobile food truck business where efficient use of space is a priority. You don't want to add a bulky cash register to an already confined space of the truck.

A POS system is a simple mobile unit, at times no bigger than the palm of your hand.

• Data on the POS system is stored in the cloud. You can access it anywhere, anytime. Are you at home dining with your loved ones when you wish to quickly check your sales for the day? You don't have to walk all the way to the main system in your truck. You can just pull up the data on your phone.

• Do you want to increase your contacts for your email marketing campaign? How about getting more tips on each order? Your POS system will do all the work. Without sounding needy, it will encourage your customers to tip or add an email ID/phone number after/before the transaction.

Setting up a POS system is easy, especially for a food truck. It will be up and running in a matter of hours. The hardware is a one-time investment, and the software is usually subscription-based. The prices and features may vary depending on the brand you choose to go with. The most popular features include:

• User-friendly interface

• Doesn't need an internet connection to operate

• Cloud storage (needs the internet)

• Compatibility with multiple operating systems

• Upselling options (registration, tips)

• Customer-facing screen

• Card reader and barcode reader

Using Mobile Apps for Orders and Payments

A POS system is more than worth it if you have a decent customer base. What if you're just starting out in the food truck industry? You can install a POS to show your customers you don't hesitate to spend on the good things for your business or just to be prepared for the best outcome. However, opt for a POS only if you have invested in everything else and there's still enough money left. Consider it as the very last thing to buy while starting a new food truck business.

If you don't have any funds left to purchase a POS system, should you settle for the age-old system of manual tallying with pen and paper? Not quite. Technology will come to your rescue again. There are a number of smartphone apps that emulate a POS system, many of which are free. The only drawback is that you will have access to only the basic features like orders and payments (including scanning cards and codes).

• Block (formerly Square)

• Loyverse

• Lightspeed

• Shopify POS

• Paypal Zettle

You can upgrade to the paid version to unlock all the available features. However, installing dedicated hardware (screens, keyboards) for your food truck's POS is only recommended when you have a steady stream of customers.

Utilizing Food Truck Location Apps

Imagine you parked your food truck in location A on the first day at noon. One of your customers loved your offerings and decided to visit you again the next day. However, the following day, at noon, you parked in location B in an attempt to explore your profits there. How will your customers know where to find you? You cannot hope to get their phone numbers on the very first day to directly send them your location. In the initial stages, staying in one location isn't a good idea either.

Food truck location apps will solve your dilemma. People who love eating at food trucks know their favorite joints will often be on the move. They sign up on location apps to be able to reach their preferred trucks at any given time of the day or night. If your truck is listed on those apps, your regular customers can find you during working hours. It is also an excellent way to expand your customer base. Anyone looking for a food truck nearby will see your location if you are in the vicinity. A few additional benefits of those apps include:

• Updating your live location.

• Sending message updates of your location to regular customers.

• Letting new customers discover you.

• Sending automatic location updates on your social media channels.

• Potential to get hired as a food truck caterer.

Currently, as of this writing, two of the best food truck location apps are *"Roaming Hunger"* and *"Truck Spotting."*

Taking Advantage of Marketing Tech

Gone are the days of limited marketing options for businesses. Paying a lot of money for television commercials is a thing of the past. Today, you are spoiled for choice, especially in the world of technology. Most of the stuff is free, and feature-packed upgrades are downright cheap compared to traditional ads. For the restaurant business, including food trucks, the marketing options are innumerable.

Even if you have already embraced technological advancements like email marketing and social media, it's time to take them to the next level with these cutting-edge apps and tools.

• **Appy Pie:** Location updates, menu display, food orders, loyalty program.

• **Mailchimp:** One of the first bulk mailing platforms. It allows for location updates, food truck information, surveys, and schedules.

• **TextMagic:** Send bulk messages that can include anything from location updates to menu changes.

Displaying a Digital Menu

A physical menu book is expected at food trucks. Do the un-expected instead. Awe your customers with a digital menu. It is similar to a customer-side screen in a POS without the entire setup. It can be static or interactive, depending on your requirements. A few of the leading-edge digital menu platforms include:

• **ScreenCloud**: A signage app that you can use to display a static menu on a screen. Upload your menu to the cloud and cast it on the screen for customers to browse through.

• **NEC Display Solutions:** This brand provides everything you need to display your menu, from a dedicated screen to customized templates.

• **ElectroMenu:** This is a specialized menu display system. Opting for additional features will also transform it into a compact POS system.

Providing Delivery Options

Say it's a slow afternoon, and you don't have any customers. There aren't even any prospects visible for miles in either direction. Then, you receive a call from a regular, saying they cannot make it to your truck, but if you could drive down to their house, they will make it worth your while. You will immediately take them up on the offer.

However, if you had received the same call during peak hours, you would have wished you had a delivery person at hand. What if you had received multiple such calls asking to deliver? You can't hope to employ several dedicated delivery people at once, at least not when you are just starting off.

The best way to tackle this eventuality is to register for a delivery app. It takes care of everything from the delivery point of view, from collecting the order to placing it on their doorstep. It's like a side business where you barely need to do anything but focus on your main task of handling your in-person customers. Three apps stand out in the world of food delivery in the US.

1. DoorDash: It is the largest food delivery company in the country.

2. Uber Eats: This platform recently gathered steam thanks to its fast service times since the deliveries are done by Uber drivers themselves.

3. Grubhub: It is the oldest food delivery platform in this list. Founded in 2004, it has some of the most efficient delivery partners.

Incorporating Sustainable Practices

When it is a question of the environment, food trucks have the potential to have one of the highest carbon footprints in the food industry. Eating on the go implies using plastic disposables (cups, plates, glasses, etc.). Furthermore, food trucks tend to keep moving from one place to another. So they are, potentially, also responsible for pollution. You can curb this by incorporating sustainable practices in your food truck business.

Sustainability is an innovative concept that has recently gained traction. In simple terms, sustainability is making the resources of your food truck last the maximum time so you can make great profits in the long run. It is about protecting the environment in which you do business so you can keep doing it for many years to come. You will be investing not only in your future but also in that of generations to come. It can't even be called an investment. It is more of a set of rules you should follow to create a sustainable food truck business.

• Buy Local Products
It's not just about supporting your local producers and vendors. It is about supporting your business by bringing down your investment in raw materials. Locally produced goods are   relatively cheaper than imported stuff. They are fresh, which enhances the flavor of your food. Imports need to be preserved to keep them fresh during the journey, and many

of the preservatives used can lead to major health problems in the future. With locally grown products, you can reduce your carbon footprint significantly by removing imported transportation as a polluting factor.

• Create a Sustainable Menu

Imagine that your menu consists of a dish that requires an ingredient (say, with a short expiry date) that none of your other offerings need. Nobody buys that dish for a few days, after which you will have to throw away the expired ingredient. This kind of food truck menu encourages wastage. A sustainable menu will have a few other dishes that require special ingredients. In fact, you need to make sure each ingredient in your inventory can be used to prepare multiple menu offerings. It will help you reduce wastage to a great degree.

• Save Fuel and Energy

Do you keep the burner on before beginning to cook a new dish? Is the exhaust fan in your kitchen running all the time? What about your truck's fuel consumption? Make sure you turn off the burner between dishes. Invest in a long-term electricity solution, like solar panels. They will save you a ton of money in the long run. Since you need to drive your food truck to different places throughout the day, you can consider switching to an alternate fuel source, like biodiesel, which will harm the environment a little less. Every effort counts as a big step in creating a sustainable workspace.

• Invest in Eco-Friendly Products

Before launching your food truck business, check if your

products are eco-friendly. Are you using plastic for packing the orders? Switch to plant-based or biodegradable packaging, such as boxes that can be recycled to make different useful products. Use metal containers or compostable cups and paper cutlery and carry bags. If you can't help but use plastic, avoid using black plastic materials because the recycling machines find it hard to sort plastic of that color. Furthermore, coffee pods may be a convenient way to serve coffee at food trucks, but they aren't beneficial for the environment.

• Waste Reduction

Did you know that over a billion tons of food is wasted every year on the planet? Restaurants and food trucks are probably the highest contributors to that waste. Reduce your contribution by recycling the remaining food or donating it to food banks. Despite having such useful options at their disposal, more than 84% of the food is still thrown away in the US. Being a food truck business, it won't take you long to haul your leftovers to a nearby food bank or soup kitchen.

The prices are slightly higher and it's a little more effort to create a sustainable food truck, but consider it as a long-term investment in the restaurant industry and in your business. The looming global warming threat can be pushed a little farther, and you can do business for a little longer just because you decided to shell out a few more bucks for sustainable equipment
and spend a little more time each day creating a sustainable environment.

Chapter 11: Overcoming Challenges and Adapting to Change

Benefits notwithstanding, running a food truck has its challenges. From seasonal fluctuations to dealing with competitive market saturation to shifting laws and regulations, owners have many reasons to apply adaptive measures to stay afloat. This chapter provides tips on not just on how to avoid common mistakes, but on how to overcome challenges and maintain a printable business despite them.

Handling Seasonal Fluctuations

Food truck companies often experience seasonal fluctuations during certain seasons. The profit lull tends to be particularly noticeable during the winter. Fortunately, there are plenty of ways to deal with this and ensure your business will bring in profits through all seasons.

Learning to Adapt to Different Weather Conditions

By equipping your truck with elements that help you and your customers handle extremely cold and hot weather, you will have more clients even during extreme weather conditions. This can include providing shelter, investing in the truck's cooling or heating systems, and more.

Bringing in Seasonal Favorites

The spring and fall are excellent occasions to introduce new items to your menu. They can be temporary or brought on throughout the following season as well. For example, items you introduce during the fall can remain through the winter if the customer response is positive. Adding these items will further entice your regular customers to engage with your business and refer to potential new clients who will be curious about your new, exciting offerings.

Naturally, you don't have to change your entire menu for one season (in fact, it's not recommended at all because it can be off-putting to your regulars), but assigning a few new ingredients can help you boost your business during the least popular season. Beyond raising profit, it will help you save money as seasonal produce always costs less than off-season ones. Keep the usual customer favorites, but look into what the locals prefer to consume during the low season and incorporate these into your menu to attract more consumers. For example, many people will reach for comfort food during the fall/winter — and if nothing else, you can always offer hot beverages as these are another cold weather favorite.

Offer Additional Benefits for the Winter
Besides warm beverages that will warm up your customers during the winter, consider selling complementary warming accessories like hoodies and beanies at low prices. This is an additional investment, but it could entice people to stand in lines outdoors in cold weather, something people don't usually like to do. Moreover, you could use these accessories to market your brand, so even if you make less money selling food, you're still investing in the future of your business. Add some inviting lights and simple decorations to create a festive atmosphere, and people will be drawn to it right away.

Shift to Delivery and Catering
Some food truck owners would just call it quits during the winter and wait until spring to reopen for business. However, this represents a significant income loss, which you can avoid

by finding constructive ways to offer your food to people. If you can't find ways to attract customers during inclement weather, consider shifting to delivery and catering for the season.

If you're stationed in one place, chances are the nearby businesses that cater to weddings, parties, and other parties throughout the year already know about your food truck. They'll be open to your offer to provide their services to them, and you'll gain more exposure and a steady stream of income even during off-seasons. You can still keep your truck at your usual locations and hire part-time employees to do deliveries. This way, you'll still be there for your regulars in case the weather lets up a little, and they decide to venture out, but you're raising your profits by catering to those who prefer to cozy up inside their homes. Or, you can contract with delivery and catering companies, so you won't be tied to specific hours when you have to do these services. Make sure you advertise your new services online to attract more clientele.

Set up Your Truck at Public Events

Public events are held throughout the entire year. Even during winter, there are tree lighting ceremonies, Christmas market openings, and many more happenings where you can offer your food to people. If you experience an income lull at your usual location, Set up your truck at these events to draw in more business. If you don't want to hire employees or contract with other companies for delivery and catering, you can always set up an event with just your truck.

Stay in Touch with Customers

Keep engaging with your customers throughout all seasons. Before each season, ask them what they like and dislike about the upcoming season, what food items they would want to see you offer during it, and any other questions you can think of that'll help you meet their needs better. The more you can cater to them during low seasons, the more new customers you'll have, and the more motivated the old ones to keep visiting your truck even when they usually wouldn't.

Make Better Use of Your Time

Another alternative is to utilize the off time to prepare for the upcoming season. You can, for example, redesign your truck to make it more efficient or invest in equipment that enables you to offer some new, exciting items. At one time or another, all food trucks need to be updated and remodeled. If you have money to invest in these innovations, start them as soon as the off-season begins so you can have your truck ready at the start of the next popular season.

Prepare for Weather Disruptions

If you're operating in an area where weather disruptions like harsh winds, thunderstorms, and other occurrences hap-pen regularly between spring and autumn, you must be prepared. A sudden weather event can damage your truck, disrupt your operations, and set your business back finan-cially for a long time. You can avoid this by weatherproofing your vehicle and, perhaps, investing in a backup location and equipment.

Stay Relevant throughout the Entire Year
Even if you can't keep your truck on the street during the off-season, you need to make sure your brand remains relevant. During this time, work on your marketing techniques and come up with ways to get your customers excited for the opening season. You can organize an event, hold giveaways, and other social media tactics to keep your brand alive in your customers' minds. Before the season starts, post a new menu to showcase what you have to offer and create buzz around your business.

Dealing with Competition

The popularity of food trucks has been steadily rising through and competition has led to market saturation. To beat your competition, you must distinguish your brand and constantly innovate. This can be particularly troublesome when you aren't operating in a steady location, but it isn't impossible. Here are some tips on how to stay ahead of the game despite the forced competition.

Know Your Competition
Learning about what your competitors do and how they perform financially doesn't stop at establishing your brand. Your competitors will innovate, and you'll have to stay on top of what they're doing. Learn who all your competitors are (this applies to both direct, like other food trucks, and indirect competition, like brick-and-mortar businesses offering similar food). Study how they're overcoming their challenges and what changes they are doing to keep their offering rele-

vant. This will help you customize your menu, set competitive prizes for unique food items, and, consequently, stand out during advertising when you need to respond to the competitor's marketing efforts.

Focus on a Unique Brand Personality

Having initially created a unique brand image doesn't mean you'll be able to remain relevant in the market forever. Another business can come up with a similar concept, except with a few innovations, instantly positioning themselves above you. This doesn't mean you have to break your budget for new extravagant marketing efforts. It just means you need to become more creative and focus on how to make your brand distinguishable again. This could be anything that resonates with new customers or something you haven't yet offered to the old ones. Offer something new that they can't get from any of your competitors, even if it's simply a fun, more appealing presentation of your food.

Improve the Quality of Your Products and Services

One of the best ways to stay ahead of the competition is to always offer the best products and services. By constantly offering higher quality service than everyone around you, you can not only meet your client's needs, but you can also showcase your superiority above the rivals. For example, if the competitors are serving food that isn't made from scratch, you can capitalize on offering fresh, scratch-made items as these will appeal more to the customers.

Go above and beyond to make sure your clients are getting their money's worth. Showing you're always there to cater to their needs builds trust and loyalty in your business. New and old customers will appreciate your efforts and will engage with your brand and spread the word to others.

Improve Delivery Time

Do you know what hungry customers appreciate even more than good food and service? Fast delivery. Whether you serve only on-site, deliver, or do catering, you'll always be working with people who are constantly pressed for time. In fact, one of the main reasons food trucks have become so popular is because they're convenient and fast. The most competitive businesses keep the time from order to delivery under 4 minutes (on-site). Aim to match this while maintaining consistent quality in product and service, and you'll be able to differentiate your business above most of its competitors.

Adapt to Market Trends

The food delivery market is fickle and tends to change. Businesses must stay on top of these changes and implement dynamic strategies to keep up with customer preferences, culinary trends, and more. Take advantage of technological advancement and continued market analyses to continually evolve your menu, cater to changing dietary needs, and experiment with different and combined flavors. Remember, your rivals will also engage in these practices, so the only way to ensure you don't lose customers to them is by doing the same.

Building Lasting Relationships

Beyond establishing trust and loyalty with customers, it's also crucial to build lasting relationships with rivals, local authorities, and suppliers. By becoming part of this extensive community, you'll stay in the loop with the newest changes and be able to meet your customer's needs despite the fierce competition in the market.

Adapting to Regulatory Changes

Over the past years, food truck businesses have had to adapt to changing regulations for various reasons. Whether it was to figure out how to deliver food and service in a way that makes customers safe or to learn how to navigate the changing regulatory landscape regarding different locations. Going forward, food truck owners are likely looking forward to even more changes, and it's crucial to learn how to adapt to them to maintain your business.

Keep up with the Postings of the Local Authorities

Food truck regulations vary based on where you live. The best way to stay up to date with local ordinances and potential restrictions is to follow what the local authorities post and advertise through different media channels. This way, you'll always know where you can park your vehicle and how long you can remain in one single location. Similarly, you can learn about temporary or permanent measures the authorities might suggest or demand (for example, the rules about mask-wearing and limiting how many people can stand in line and how far apart that were implemented during the global pandemic). Federal agencies may also dictate where and how long you can park, what services you can provide in the area, payment methods you can or should implement, and more. For example, authorities encourage more and more use of digital and contactless payment methods for the customer's safety and convenience.

Adhere to FDA Regulations

Another (regularly updated) guideline you must follow is that of the Food and Drug Administration (FDA). This simple checklist has been revised a couple of times during the past years to ensure food truck owners can operate safely among customers. Beyond the usual food safety guidelines, the list also has suggestions for improving air circulation and removing hard-to-clean surfaces. Both of these issues can be circumvented by using technological innovations that make preparing, cooking, storing, and serving food easier and safer.

Improve Safety Signage

If the local and state regulations focus on customer safety, you can improve customer awareness by posting signs reminding people of the relevant safety guidelines. Additionally, have a poster-size menu your customers can see from a distance so they can remain compliant with the aforementioned guidelines.

Scout New Locations

If the new regulation regarding your usual locations becomes too restrictive, consider scouting out new areas. Instead of sticking to the usual places like parks, college campuses, events, and markets (where the regulations are becoming stricter), find new places to park your truck. You can reach out to essential businesses and ask them if they would allow you to park in their lot so the workers would have quick access to food during lunch breaks. Some food trucks did this near healthcare institutions during the pandemic and earned many grateful customers. Or, you can park temporarily in neighborhoods and combine your search for new territory with a marketing campaign to increase your customer base. Keep your permit restrictions and local food truck regulations in mind when exploring new sites.

Pay Attention to Equipment Failure and Food Safety

The times continue to be challenging for small businesses, including food trucks. However, this doesn't mean you can slack on equipment control and food safety measures, as this is the best way to not only alienate customers but also to get on the bad side of the regulatory bodies. As regulations continue to evolve, you must count on more rigorous control measures. Moreover, equipment failure can cost you up to a week's worth of business. If you're caught operating faulty equipment, this can increase to up to a month, plus costly penalty charges. It might also cost you upfront to stay on top of your equipment and food safety, but it will save you a lot of money and time in the long run. Proper staff training is equally fundamental in minimizing downtime and avoiding penalties. By having everyone know the proper hygiene protocol, your business will be protected, and your customers will remain happy and content with your products and services.

Chapter 12: Looking Toward the Future

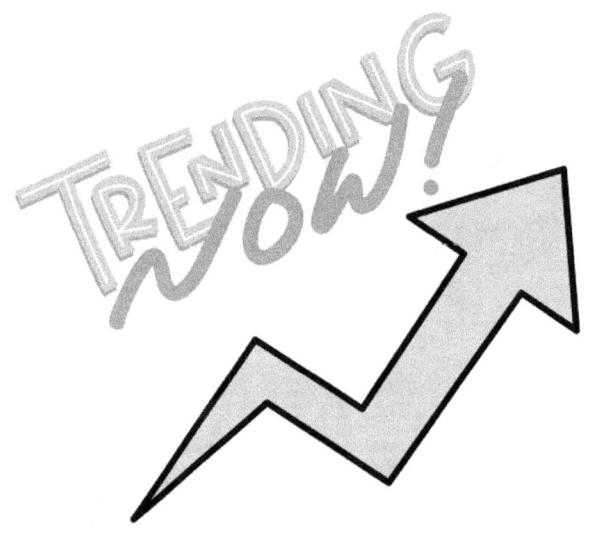

You have now gathered your resources, created your business plan, crafted your brand identity, and are ready to get started, so what's next? The future of business, especially in an industry as competitive as food, is always uncertain. That does not mean you must take a gloom-and-doom approach.

It also doesn't mean you should be overly optimistic and not make the necessary preparations in case things go wrong. The best approach when thinking about the future of your business is to be realistic, have a vision, and implement small steps toward the larger goal you are trying to achieve.

There will inevitably be roadblocks along the way, but perseverance is key. Never jump ship before weighing all your options and deeply analyzing if that would be the most appropriate move to make. Initially, your aim is to grow your business and exploit every gap that emerges in the market. Therefore, you will constantly be examining your food truck as it relates to the shifting external environment to see how you can best utilize the factors that are out of your control.

Staying motivated can be difficult, especially in hard times. Building from the ground up is frustratingly challenging, which is why most people do not have what it takes to take that path. Stay focused on the bigger picture because there are people who were once at the starting point you find yourself at with your food truck who are now making six to seven figures annually. It is not a dream if someone out there is already living it.

Emerging Trends in the Food Truck Industry

Staying on top of what is happening in the industry will help you make moves that will secure your future. Trends are forever changing, so you have to adjust your plans accordingly if you hope to achieve the highest levels of success. Trees that are too rigid when strong winds blow will snap, but the ones that bend with the storm stand right back up when it ends. Being malleable and adaptive is the only way to longevity. Take Coca-Cola, for example. Through the decades, their advertising campaigns have evolved, their bottles have changed, and their marketing strategy has been adapted according to their growth. They have remained relevant as the leading beverage company in the world. Similarly, you would need to do the same for your food truck to give you the benefits that you aim for financially and socially.

The food truck industry has been rapidly expanding over the past decade. Since 2018, the industry has grown almost 10% each year (Brophy and Rivera, 2023). With this expanding market, new opportunities have arisen, but at the same time, some saturation has occurred, which means that the barrier to entry has also increased. The projections of growth in the industry are not looking as good as they used to with some estimates stating that from 2023 to 2024 the growth will probably only be about 3-5%, unlike the previous years. (Brophy and Rivera, 2023). Market share will be tougher to compete for with less growth, so to be sustainable as a business in the food truck industry, the key is to stick out from the crowd.

Food trucks are highly competitive. No food truck currently operating has more than 5% market share. Each business is fighting for a small piece of a growing pie that is expected to be worth $2 billion by 2030. Since you cannot capture a large part of the market share as an individual food truck, your expectations should be catered to this reality. However, the budding industry is still new, so there may be a chance to create a food truck franchise that changes these dynamics if you are courageous enough to dream that big.

Most people who frequent food trucks are under the age of 45. For it to sustainably last into the future, you must appeal to a younger demographic. The reason these people are the primary consumers of food truck meals is a combination of their use of social media and their on-the-go lifestyle. Furthermore, food trucks that operate in areas where the nightlife is vibrant also contribute to bringing down the age of consumers because, typically, younger people stay out longer.

Mexican cuisine has emerged as the most popular food truck choice, with many people selling tacos, tamales, and quesadillas. The flavorful food is easy to make with cost-effective ingredients. That, coupled with demand, is most likely the reason Mexican food is thriving in the food truck scene. This information can be used in two ways: either you can jump on the wave of the popularity of Mexican food, or you can distance yourself from it so that your food truck can stand out more in the market. Mexican food may be at the peak of its popularity, so it is necessary to look into other options that are on the rise to remain relevant in the future.

Portland, Orlando, Indianapolis, Denver, and Philadelphia are some of the cities where food trucks are the most popular. For longevity, you can either set up in a city with a well-established culture of food trucks, or you can try to create demand in a different city where they are not as popular. If you are looking for popularity in a city where food trucks are not as common, you need to choose a location with many young people because they are your most likely customers.

New food trucks cost about $125,000–$200,000, and second-hand food trucks, on average, cost in the range of $30,000–$70,000. You could probably cut some more costs if you have the skills to do the conversion from a regular van yourself. These prices are important to know because they are your largest investment. Also, if you have to sell your truck for whatever reason, you should know the retail value so you can assess the startup costs you can recoup if your business fails. Thinking about failure is not pessimism. It allows you to prepare for the worst-case scenarios. No one can fully predict the future so you do not know what can arise in the market or your personal life that prompts the sale of your food truck. Moreover, knowing the average cost of second-hand food trucks can help you plan if you want to sell to upgrade the business as you grow.

Employee wages in the food truck industry take just over a quarter of the money the business earns. On average, there are about 1.2 employees per food truck. The number of people employed in the industry is also shooting up, with the growth rate of employment in food trucks climbing by just over 8% over five years. For your business to be sustainable, you will need to consider the employment environment especially as you are expanding. If you are aiming to own more than one food truck, you will need employees because you and your partners, if you have any, will not be able to be everywhere all at once.

Realistically, from a purely statistical point of view, it is more likely that your food truck will fail than succeed. Within the first three years of business, about 60% of food trucks meet their end. The uncertainty of the food industry means that you will have to do a lot of work to last more than three years. You must be prepared for a tumultuous and slow journey.

Expansion and Scaling Your Business

Considering the uncertainty of the industry, scaling and expanding a food truck business can quickly become complicated. Before you take any step to expand, you must make sure that you are ready. Biting off more than you can chew could mean the destruction of a profitable business. First, make sure that you are comfortable with your food truck and that it has reached a level of success that can act as a safety net if your expansion is not successful. You need to assess whether you have built a strong and loyal customer base. You also need to analyze if your brand identity is strong enough to keep growing.

Market research is the foundation of scaling your business. Speak to your customers and ask them what you can improve and what they would like to see more of. This will guide your scaling operation. Somebody may comment that they want more varieties of a certain menu item or would visit you more in a different location. These answers will shape the decisions you make to expand your business and can be enlightening by highlighting factors that you never thought about. The best feedback comes from the people already supporting your business because it is in their interest to help you do better. You can also do market research with online surveys, as well as in-person surveys, in areas that you would like to target.

Expanding and scaling your business needs an ironclad plan. Your entire vision for where you want the business to be in the next five to ten years should be outlined. Every aspect must be covered, including your team, investors, and stake-holders, while detailing exactly which actions you will take to get you to the next level. Without a clear plan, you will find your head spinning with no solid direction. When your business plan is constructed containing meticulous details, you will know when you are deviating from the path, or if your plan needs adjusting because it is not working how you thought it would.

You need capital to expand your food truck business. This can come from several places, including savings, invest-ments, or loans. No two situations are the same, so you need to figure out what is best for you. There are pros and cons to all these capital-generating strategies, so weigh your business according to your vision and needs to see what will work best. The capital you require should be outlined in your business plan. To minimize the risk of misappropriating your resources, calculations for everything must be done long before you attempt to acquire funds.

As soon as people hear paperwork, they shut down. This is an overlooked yet important part of any business. Imagine having a thriving food truck just for the authorities to shut it down because you did not have the correct licenses and permits. Laws differ in various regions, so it is important to conduct thorough research and make sure that all the legal requirements are met. This may include licenses for food and drinks, as well as permits to trade in public.

Starting your business is only the first step. You may think that a food truck only requires you to get the ingredients, prepare them, and market the business, but maintenance is essential. Your equipment and vehicle will have to be periodically repaired and serviced. Furthermore, health standards must be up to par with the laws and codes of the city you operate within. If you're using chairs, tables, and decorations to create an atmosphere, they will also need to be regularly updated and repaired as they age. Before you expand, think about the additional maintenance costs that will be required and if with those charges your business will still be viable. Moreover, your technology would also need to be upgraded as you go. A pen and a book may work for tracking your finances in the beginning, but that quickly becomes counterintuitive and obsolete. Neglecting technological advancement in whatever way it shows up is a huge hindrance to your progression.

Lastly, you need a great team. Nobody is perfect. You have your strengths and weaknesses like anybody else. A carefully selected team can make up for your shortfalls and take your business to where you want it to be. You may be a visionary creative who is amazing at coming up with new recipes but is lacking in the organizational and logistics departments. You could be a great leader and motivator, but you have no clue how online marketing works. Honest self-analysis allows you to see what you are missing so that you can bring the right people in to help launch you from the ground level.

Remember that patience and consistency are the key pillars of business success. Your food truck is not going to spontaneously manifest into the glorious vision you have for it overnight. The road is long and full of obstacles. Take one step at a time and meet the challenges head-on as they pop up. You may need to slow down at times or take a few steps back to regroup, but in these moments, as impossible as it seems, try not to be discouraged and keep pushing forward.

Inspirational Stories for Aspiring Entrepreneurs

This chapter might have seemed overly discouraging so far. But don't let that deter you! The primary aim of this operations manual has been to present you with a comprehensive view of the facts—both the positive and the challenging aspects. In reality, the food truck industry is filled with numerous success stories. Ordinary food truck owners are enjoying a fulfilling livelihood by pursuing their passion. Regrettably, a significant number of individuals enter the business without adequate preparation and information, leading to approximately half of food trucks facing failure within the initial three years, But bear in mind that with the knowledge gained from this book alone, you are already significantly ahead of the curve. Here are some success stories to proof the tremendous success you can obtain in this business:

The Roll-up Food Truck, started by a dedicated team of entrepreneurs in Colorado, has grown to generate $600,000 annually. The gourmet eggroll business was started in 2018 with a $2,700 trailer in Widefield. With a startup cost of $8,000, they managed to grow into the successful and popular brand they are today. Their digital marketing strategy, coupled with a community-centered approach, propelled the food truck from humble beginnings into a successful and sustainable business.

Corbin and Taylor channeled their passion for craft beer into a mobile business called Tap Truck USA, which is earning them $360,000 per year. They constructed a vintage truck affectionately named "Bae" and started trading in San Diego. They began with an initial investment of $50,000 and, in only four years, managed to significantly grow until they established 45 locations nationwide. Their vision is to spread into the international market. From the looks of things, they are well on their way there.

Kyle Gourlie, or "The Vet Chef," is a retired military veteran who suffered a brain injury forcing him out of active duty. He decided to start selling Mexican food out of a large truck. With the support of his wife and delicious recipes from his father-in-law, Gourlie managed to grow his business to the point where he is earning $400,000 annually. He is motivated by a higher mission to help veterans reintegrate into civilian life, so the business is entirely run by ex-military people. Not only has he managed to build a profitable business, but he is changing the lives of many people who need it in the process.

When you remind yourself of the success stories, you can gain the motivation you need to bravely dive into this uncertain journey.

Conclusion

When it comes to the opportunities you get by running a food truck, the sky's the limit. As you've learned from this book, the food truck business has its challenges, but as both history and current market analysis show, it is a business with a reliable market demand. The key to success here is learning how to cater to that demand. One of the factors that will help you achieve that is creating a valid concept. That will be your unique selling point. The next choice you'll have to make is whether to purchase, lease, or rent your truck. Having acquired the truck, you can start refining your concept by coming up with a catchy name, logo, tagline, and mission statement for your business. Don't forget about designing the truck's interior layout either, as this will be based on your menu concept (and the equipment you need). Once you know where you'll prepare, cook, and store food, it's time to put your items on the menu. Remember, you'll need to think about the logistics of sourcing and addressing different dietary needs and allergies while coming up with a unique and profitable menu.

To start engaging with customers, you'll first need to attract them. You can do this by building a strong online presence through a blog, website, or social media. The latter represents an excellent opportunity for cost-efficient marketing and promotion tactics, so you should take advantage of it as much as possible. Beyond advertising your brand by your-self, you can reach out to content creators and collaborate with them so they can promote your brand, too.

Management represents another crucial aspect of running a successful business, and as you've learned, proper staff re-cruitment and training can make it much easier to establish an efficient workflow in your kitchen. Other steps you can take are developing efficient time management, inventory control, and supply chain management techniques. Tech-nological innovations like using a top-grade POS system or converting your mobile device into one will also help your business run smoothly.

Other aspects tackled by this book were choosing the opti-mal location and getting into catering by participating in re-gional catering events. These are crucial for improving your brand's visibility and creating awareness and recognition. Still, even with all these helpful tactics, you might run into some difficulties — which is why the book has a specific chapter dedicated to them and how to overcome them. By learning about these and the future aspects of the food truck industry, you can make informed decisions. It's a demanding feat, and you might experience ups and downs, but don't let that deter you from pursuing your goal. If establishing a food truck business is your dream, go ahead and start making it into a reality. After all, you're now richer with all this valuable knowledge you've gained from this book. It's up to you to start using it to your advantage.

Appendix

Sample Business Plan

Kitchen to Curb
Business Plan

Elliot M. Sage, Owner

TIP: Choose a business name that is memorable. One that reflects your brand and and is easy to relate to the type of cuisine or service you offer.

EXECUTIVE SUMMARY

The goal of the executive summary is to encourage readers to delve deeper into your business plan. It serves as a snapshot of your entire plan. Make it engaging, informative, and reflective of the passion you have for your food truck venture. It should be a brief overview, so keep each element concise and to the point. Use language that captures the reader's interest. Highlight what makes your food truck business exciting and worth investing in.

TIP: Although the Executive Summary appears at the beginning of your business plan, it's often easier to write the executive summary last. This way, you can summarize key points after you've developed the rest of the plan.

TIP: Edit it carefully. Since it's the first section many readers will see, ensure your executive summary is well-edited and free of errors. It should present a polished and professional image of your business.

Example: Kitchen to Curb is a mobile food venture dedicated to providing high-quality, delicious [cuisine type] on the go. We pride ourselves on the quality, freshness and unique flavors. With a commitment to culinary excellence and customer satisfaction, we aim to deliver a unique dining experience through our vibrant and conveniently located food truck.

MISSION STATEMENT

(Concise statement outlining the purpose and values of your food truck business)

Example: Our mission is to bring joy to the taste buds of our customers by offering flavorful and innovative [cuisine type] dishes served with speed and convenience. We strive to create a memorable dining experience that captures the essence of our passion for great food and exceptional service.

BUSINESS CONCEPT

(Describe your food truck concept, including type of cuisine, target market and unique selling points)

Example: Kitchen to Curb specializes in [specific cuisine] cuisine, focusing on fresh, locally sourced ingredients to create a menu that caters to a diverse range of tastes. Our mobile kitchen is equipped to serve customers at various urban locations, events, and gatherings, providing an accessible and enjoyable alternative to traditional dining options.

MARKET ANALYSIS

(Describe your ideal customers, including demographics and preferences)

Example: *The food truck industry is experiencing significant growth due to changing consumer preferences for convenient, diverse, and unique dining experiences. Our target market includes busy professionals, event attendees, and food enthusiasts seeking a delicious and convenient meal option. We have identified key locations and events with high foot traffic to maximize our market reach. Growing demand for diverse and unique food options, increased popularity of food trucks at events and festivals.*

UNIQUE SELLING PROPOSITION (USP)

(Anything that makes you special or better than the competition)

Example: *What sets Kitchen to Curb apart is our dedication to culinary excellence, using fresh and locally sourced ingredients to craft unique and memorable dishes. Our efficient and customer-friendly service, combined with a vibrant and inviting food truck design, ensures a positive and unforgettable experience for every customer.*

TIP: Focus on what your specific customer base in your specific operating area care about (is it speed of service, pricing, variety? etc.)

PRODUCT AND SERVICES

(List the items on your menu, including pricing and any signature dishes. Also highlight any unique features of your food truck, such as special recipes, dietary accommodations, or seasonal offerings)

Example: *Our main menu includes a curated selection of [list Cuisine Type details] dishes, emphasizing freshness, quality, and affordability. Our Catering Services include customizable catering packages for private and corporate events.*

OPERATIONAL PLAN

(Outline short-term and long-term objectives and your plans to achieve them)

Example: *Our objective is to strengthen our supply chain by establishing relationships with local suppliers for fresh ingredients. Continue to research and secure high-traffic locations and participate in local events. Our food truck design is a vibrant and eye-catching design to attract customers.*

MARKETING AND SALES STRATEGY

(You msy describe your brand identity, including logo, colors, and overall aesthetic. Outline your marketing strategies, including online and offline methods, and how you sell your products)

Example: *Kitchen to Curb has established a strong online* *presence through social media marketing, a user-friendly website, and online ordering. Through local partnerships, we've initiated collaborations with local businesses for cross-promotions. We have also expanded our reach with Loyalty Programs to encourage repeat business*

FINANCIAL PLAN
(Outline financial details)
Example: *Kitchen to Curb start-up costs of [$$$] include initial investment in the food truck, kitchen equipment, licenses, and permits. Operating Expenses [$$$] include monthly costs for ingredients, fuel, maintenance, and marketing. Our revenue streams derive from sales from the food truck, catering services, and potential partnerships.*

TEAM
(You and whoever else may be on the staff)
Example: *Elliot Sage is the founder/owner and manager. Additional culinary team members includes an experienced chef with expertise in [Cuisine Type] and two friendly service staff.*

FINANCIAL PROJECTIONS
(Financial outlook)
Example: *Kitchen to Curb anticipates steady revenue growth over the next three years, driven by increased brand recognition, expanding our customer base in our areas of*

operation, and diversifying revenue streams, including the addition of new menu offerings.

RISK ANALYSIS

(Identify any market, operational, and/or financial risk associated with your food truck business)
Example: *Natural inherent risks include competition and changing consumer preferences, equipment malfunction, fluctuations in ingredient prices and economic downturns.*

CONCLUSION

Kitchen to Curb is poised to become a prominent player in the local food scene, offering a unique and flavorful experience for customers on the go. With a focus on quality, convenience, and customer satisfaction, we anticipate steady growth and success in the dynamic and growing food truck industry.

TIP: Remember to tailor each section to your specific business and market conditions, and consider seeking professional advice for financial projections and legal requirements. Also, you can learn more about business plans and download actual examples by visiting the Small Business Administration at https://www.sba.gov/

National and Selected Regional Food Truck Associations

National Food Truck Association
https://nationalfoodtrucks.org/
Charlotte Food Truck Association
https://charlottefoodtrucks.org/index.html
Central Ohio Food Truck Association
https://www.centralohiofoodtrucks.org/
Cincinnati Food Truck Association
https://cincinnatifoodtruckassociation.org/events
Connecticut Food Truck Association
https://ctfoodassociation.org/
District Maryland Virginia Food Truck Association
https://www.facebook.com/DMVFTA/
Florida Food Truck Association
https://www.facebook.com/FloridaFoodTruckAssociation/
Food Truck Association of Georgia
https://www.foodtruckassociationofgeorgia.com/
Grand Rapids Food Truck Association
https://www.foodtrucksgr.com/
Greater Lehigh Valley Mobile Food Alliance
https://glvmobilefood.org/

Greater Pittsburgh Food Truck Association
http://gpfta.com/

Greater Spokane Food Trucks
https://greaterspokanefoodtrucks.com/
Houston Area Food Truck Association
http://www.hafta.us/
Illinois Food Truck Association
https://illinoisfoodtruckassociation.wordpress.com/

Indiana Mobile Food Vendor Association
https://www.facebook.com/IMFVA.ORG/
Kansas Food Truckk Association
https://kcfoodtrucks.com/kansas-city-food-truck-locations/
Maryland Mobile Food Vending Association
https://www.facebook.com/MDMFVA/
Memphis Food Truck Alliance
https://memphisfoodtruckers.org/
Midessa Mobile Food Vendors Aoociation
https://prestigefoodtrucks.com/home/client-testimonials/midessa-mobile-food-vendors-association-food-truck/
Minnesota Food Truck Association
https://mnfoodtruckassociation.org/
Nashville Food Truck Association
https://www.facebook.com/nashvillefta/
New Jersey Food Truck Association
https://njfta.org/
New York Food Truck Association
https://nyfta.org/members
New Orleans Food Trucks
http://www.nolafoodtrucks.com/

North Texas Food Truck Association
https://www.ntxfta.org/

Omaha Food Truck Association
https://www.facebook.com/omahafta/
Oregon Food Truck Association
https://oregonfoodtruckassociation.com/
Philly Mobile Food Association
https://www.facebook.com/phillymfa/
Queen City Mobile Food Truck Association
https://www.qcmfta.com/
Richmond Food Truck Association
https://richmondfoodtruckassociation.com/book
San Antonio Food Truck Association
https://www.facebook.com/SAFoodTruckAssn/
South Shore Food Truck Association
https://www.facebook.com/southshorefoodtruckassoci-
ation/
Southern California Mobile Food Vendors
http://socalmfva.com/
St. Louis Food Truck Association
https://www.stlfta.com/
Syracuse Food Truck Association
https://syrfoodtrucks.com/

Tallahassee Food Truck Association
https://www.tallyfta.com/portfolio/the-cake-shop
Washington State Food Trucks
https://wafoodtrucks.org/king-county

Glossary of Terms

Commissary: A licensed commercial kitchen where food truck owners prepare and store food, as required by health regulations.

Cuisine: A style or method of cooking, especially as characteristic of a particular country, region, or establishment.

Food Truck Finder Apps: Mobile applications that help customers locate nearby food trucks, providing information on their current locations, menus, and schedules.

Loyalty Program: A marketing strategy that rewards customers for repeat business, often through points, discounts, or free items.

POS (Point of Sale) System: A system used to complete sales transactions and manage various business operations, including payment processing and inventory tracking.

SWOT Analysis: An acronym for Strengths, Weaknesses, Opportunities, and Threats. A strategic planning tool used to identify and analyze these factors in a business.

Market Analysis: An assessment of market conditions, including target demographics, competitors, and trends, to inform business decisions.

Branding: The process of creating a unique and recognizable identity for a business, including elements like logos, colors, and messaging.

<u>Permits and Licensing</u>: Legal permissions required to operate a food truck, including health permits, business licenses, and parking permits.

<u>Target Market</u>: The specific group of customers at which a product or service is aimed. Identifying and understanding the target market is crucial for effective marketing.

<u>Break-even Analysis</u>: The point at which total revenue equals total expenses, resulting in neither profit nor loss.

<u>Revenue Projections</u>: Predictions of future income based on expected sales and business performance.

<u>SWOT Analysis:</u> An analysis of a business's internal strengths and weaknesses, along with external opportunities and threats, to inform strategic planning.

<u>Mobile Payment Processing</u>: Systems that enable businesses to accept payments through mobile devices, including credit/debit card transactions.

<u>Inventory Management</u>: The process of monitoring and controlling the stock of goods a business sells, including ordering, storage, and tracking.

<u>Social Media Management</u>: The use of tools and strategies to manage and optimize a business's presence on social media platforms.

<u>Food Truck Associations:</u> Organizations or groups that support and represent the interests of food truck owners, providing networking opportunities and resources.

<u>Pitch:</u> A brief presentation or description of a business idea, often used when seeking investors or partnerships.

<u>Financial Projections:</u> Forecasts of a business's future financial performance, including income statements, balance sheets, and cash flow statements.

<u>Marketing Plan:</u> A comprehensive document outlining a business's marketing strategy, including target audience, channels, and promotional activities.

References

4 Seasonal Changes to Your Food Truck to Grow Business. (2021, July 13). California Cart Builder. https://californiacartbuilder.com/4-seasonal-changes-to-your-food-truck-to-grow-business/

Bartoszek, D. (2023, October 24). How much does a Food Truck cost in 2023? UpMenu. https://www.upmenu.com/blog/how-much-does-a-food-truck-cost/

Battla, N. (2023, August 22). Building a Resilient Business: Risk Management for Food Truck Operators. Linkedin.Com. https://www.linkedin.com/pulse/building-resilient-business-risk-management-food-truck-nadeem-battla/

Battla, N. (2023, April 24). Ride the Wave: Thriving in the Food Truck Industry Amidst Changing Locations and Seasons. Linkedin.Com. https://www.linkedin.com/pulse/ride-wave-thriving-food-truck-industry-amidst-changing-nadeem-battla/

Bishop, B. (2023, May 17). Why are food trucks so popular? Culinary entrepreneurs in Wabash weigh in. Visit Wabash County. https://www.visitwabashcounty.com/why-are-food-trucks-so-popular/

Choosing   the   Right   Equipment   and   Supplies   for   Your   Food   Truck.   Myaifrontdesk.Com
. https://www.myaifrontdesk.com/blog/choosing-the-right
-equipment-and-supplies-for-your-food-truck

Daltontomich.com. https://daltontomich.com/top-5-legal-c
onsiderations-facing-food-truck-owners/

Dillon, M. (2022, February 14). 6 best types of Eco-friendly
food packaging (and 4 to avoid). Meyers; The Meyers Printing
Companies, Inc. https://meyers.com/meyers-blog/eco-frien
dly-food-packaging/

Efinancialmodels.com. https://www.efinancialmodels.com/
creating-a-business-plan-for-your-food-truck-business/

Food truck business plan template. PandaDoc. https://www
.pandadoc.com/food-truck-business-plan-template/

Food   Truck   Design.   WebstaurantStore. https://www.webstaurantstore.com/article/487/
food-truck-design-and-layout.html

Food Truck Industry Trends and Statistics in 2024. (2023). T
oasttab.com. https://pos.toasttab.com/blog/on-the-line/fo
od-truck-industry-trends-and-statistics

Food   Truck   Owners   Use   The   Seasonal   Market.   (2021,   December   13).   ZenBusiness
Inc. https://www.zenbusiness.com/blog/5-ways-for-food-tr
ucks-to-take-advantage-of-the-seasonal-market/

FoodTruckr. (2014, January 15). How to Start a Food Truck 02:
Decide What You'll Sell. FoodTruckr | How to Start and Run a

Successful Food Truck Business |. https://foodtruckr.com/how-to-start-a-food-truck/start-food-truck-decide-youll-sell/

FoodTruckr. (2019, March 16). Properly managing your time as A food truck owner. FoodTruckr | How to Start and Run a Successful Food Truck Business |; FoodTruckr | How to Start and Run a Successful Food Truck Business. https://foodtruckr.com/business/properly-managing-your-time-as-a-food-truck-owner/

FTB. (2021, October 20). Starting a Food Truck: 3 Challenges a Food Truck Owner must overcome. Foodtruckbooking.com . https://www.foodtruckbooking.us/news/1094/starting-a-food-truck-3-challenges-a-food-truck-owner-must-overcome

Google Business Profile – Get Listed on Google.https://www.google.com/intl/en_eg/business/

Hastings, A. (2023, September 28). 6 ways to get your food truck into festivals. Food Liability Insurance Program. https://www.fliprogram.com/blog/6-ways-to-get-your-food-truck-into-festivals

Hayes, A. (2010, August 16). What is a POS system, and how does it work? Investopedia. https://www.investopedia.com/terms/p/point-of-sale.asp

Hightower, S. (2022, March 7). How to Navigate Changing Food Truck Regulations. Heart & Hustle. https://www.spoton.com/blog/navigate-changing-food-truck-regulations/

How do you measure the impact of brand identity and positioning on customer loyalty? https://www.linkedin.com/advice/0/how-do-you-measure-impact-brand-identity-positioning

How to Scale Your Pop-Up or Food Truck to a Brick-and-Mortar Restaurant. Toasttab.com . https://pos.toasttab.com/blog/on-the-line/how-to-scale-popup-food-truck-brick-mortar-restaurant

How to Start a Food Truck. WebstaurantStore. https://www.webstaurantstore.com/article/458/start-a-food-truck.html

Hudson, E. (2023, August 24). The Ultimate Guide to Marketing Strategies & How to Improve Your Digital Presence. Hubspot. https://blog.hubspot.com/marketing/digital-strategy-guide

Kewalramani, N. (2021, August 26). 6 Tips To Rock Food Truck Branding. The Restaurant Times. https://www.posist.com/restaurant-times/usa/food-truck-branding-ideas.html

Krook, D. (2019, December 20). The history of the food truck. TouchBistro. https://www.touchbistro.com/blog/the-history-of-the-food-truck/

Larson, S. (2022, December 16). How to choose the best location for your food truck. Escoffier. https://www.escoffier.edu/blog/food-entrepreneurship/how-to-choose-the-best-location-for-your-food-truck/

Lavinsky, D. (2023, February 22). Sample business plan for a food truck business. Growthink. https://www.growthink.com/businessplan/help-center/sample-business-plan-for-a-food-truck-business legionfoodtrucks. (2023, January 11). A Guide to Selecting Equipment for a Food Truck. Legion Food Trucks. https://legionfoodtrucks.com/food-truck-equipment/a-guide-to-selecting-equipment-for-a-food-truck/

legionfoodtrucks. (2023, September 28). Ultimate Guide To Food Truck Branding. Legion Food Trucks. https://legionfoodtrucks.com/food-truck-business-plan/ultimate-guide-to-food-truck-branding/

Making the Right Choice: How to Decide Whether to Buy, Rent, or Lease a Food Truck. (2023, April 12). Octopos. https://octopos.com/how-to-decide-whether-to-buy-rent-or-lease-a-food-truck/

McCarthy, D. (2016, November 21). 6 Benefits of a Food Truck business over a traditional restaurant. The Restaurant Times. https://www.posist.com/restaurant-times/restro-gyaan/5-reasons-why-you-should-open-a-food-truck-instead-of-a-regular-restaurant.html

McCarthy, D. (2021, October 28). How your food truck can make the best of food festivals in 2022. The Restaurant Times. https://www.posist.com/restaurant-times/restro-gyaan/leverage-food-festivals-food-trucks.html

McCarthy, D. (2021, October 29). Setting up A sustainable food truck in 2023. The Restaurant Times. https://www.posist.com/restaurant-times/restro-gyaan/setting-sustainable-food-truck.html

Mendadala, R. (2018, March 7). Supply chain management: Truck operations management. Fayetteville Technical Community College. https://www.faytechcc.edu/academics/business-programs/supply-chain-management-truck-operations-management/

Morgan, B. (2015, November 22). 10 Tips for Running a Food Truck - businessnewsdaily.com. Business News Daily; businessnewsdaily.com. https://www.businessnewsdaily.com/8595-food-truck-tips.html

Myrick, R. (2016, April 27). Beating The Competition In The Food Truck Industry. Mobile Cuisine | Food Truck, Pop Up & Street Food Coverage. https://mobile-cuisine.com/business/beating-the-competition/

Myrick, R. (2016, March 26). Determine your food truck's staffing needs. Dummies. https://www.dummies.com/article/business-careers-money/business/small-business/general-small-business/determine-your-food-trucks-staffing-needs-171910/

Myrick, R. (2020, April 13). 5 food truck staff training tips. Mobile Cuisine | Food Truck, Pop Up & Street Food Coverage; Mobile Cuisine, LLC. https://mobile-cuisine.com/human-resources/5-food-truck-staff-training-tips/

Myrick, R. (2020, February 11). Validating Your Food Truck Concept. Mobile Cuisine | Food Truck, Pop Up & Street Food Coverage. https://mobile-cuisine.com/startup-basics/validating-food-truck-concept/

Nelson, L. (2016, April 14). Think you're eating local food? It might be a lie. Vox. https://www.vox.com/2016/4/14/11431 974/local-farmers-market-farm-to-table-lie

Peek, S. (2019, January 9). How to Start a Food Truck Business. Business News Daily; businessnewsdaily.com . https://www.businessnewsdaily.com/9237-how-to-start-f ood-truck-business.html

Pendrill, K. (2022, April 8). 5 restaurant supply chain manage-ment best practices and tips. TouchBistro. https://www.tou chbistro.com/blog/restaurant-supply-chain-management/

Perkins, R. (2020, November 9). 5 pro tips for cre-ating a unique food truck menu. Delivery Con-cepts. https://deliveryconcepts.com/5-pro-tips-for-creating -a-unique-food-truck-menu/

Perkins, R. (2022, January 10). Owning a Food Truck: The Pros and Cons. Prestige Food Trucks. https://prestigefoodtrucks .com/2022/01/owning-a-food-truck-the-pros-and-cons/

QSR Magazine. (2022, September 2). 4 tips to successfully scale your food truck business. QSR Magazine. https://www .qsrmagazine.com/growth/fast-casual/outside-insights-18/

Rivera, A. (2017, October 19). Food truck tech you need to know about. Business.com. https://www.business.com/arti cles/food-truck-technology-guide/

Rivera, D. (2023, October 24). 8 best POS apps & mobile POS systems. Fit Small Business. https://fitsmallbusiness.com/b est-pos-apps/

Rivera, D., & Brophy, M. (2023, September 8). Top 20 food truck industry statistics. Fit Small Business. https://fitsmallbusiness.com/food-truck-industry-statistics/

Smith, M. (2023, November 4). Social Media for Food Trucks: A Brand-Building Guide. Constant Contact. https://www.constantcontact.com/blog/social-media-for-food-trucks/

Strikingly. (2022, October 2). 8-Step Plan to Start a Food Truck Business. https://www.strikingly.com/content/blog/food-truck-business/

Stubbs , A. T. (2019, February 21). Stubbs, A. T. 3 must-have technologies when opening food trucks. Softwareadvice.com. https://www.softwareadvice.com/resources/opening-food-trucks/

Stumpf, J. (2023, October 23). How to start a food truck: the inside scoop. CloudKitchens. https://cloudkitchens.com/blog/how-to-start-a-food-truck/

The 4 most profitable delivery apps for food trucks. (2023, November 30). Tryotter. https://tryotter.com/blog/restaurant-toolkit/most-profitable-delivery-apps-food-trucks

Traylor, R. (2020, October 5). How to: Launching a food truck catering business. Www.foodtruckoperator.com. https://www.foodtruckoperator.com/articles/how-to-launching-a-food-truck-catering-business/

Walls, P. (2022, April 7). 13 food truck success stories [2023]. Starterstory.com; Starter Story. https://www.starterstory.com/ideas/food-truck/success-stories

What is Brand Positioning and Why is it Important? (2023, December 15). Amazon Ads. https://advertising.amazon.co m/library/guides/brand-positioning

Why are Food Trucks so popular? | Shortys Food Truck. (2022, June 28) https://shortysfoodtruck.com.au/shortys-fo od-blog/why-are-food-trucks-so-popular/

About the Author

With over two decades of experience as an Entrepreneur and Education Consultant, I have had the privilege of aiding clients and students across various specialized domains, including finance, business start-up and management, real estate, and federal and state tax law.

Without a doubt, my deep-seated passion lies in the realm of teaching, where I relish the opportunity to impart practical and invaluable knowledge to eager learners, opening doors to entrepreneurial business opportunities, fresh concepts and innovative ideas.

If you've derived any benefit from this manual and enjoyed reading it, please consider posting a review. I'm always happy to hear your comments and suggestions.

Click here   or scan the QR code below to leave your honest review.

SCAN HERE!